SIMPLE MAN'S DREAMS

STORIES OF THE HUNT

VOL. 2

VICTOR SCARINZI

INKS & BINDINGS

Copyright © 2023 by Victor Scarinzi

ISBN: 979-8-88615-170-1 (Paperback)

The views expressed in this book are solely those of the author and do not necessarily reflect the views of the publisher, and the publisher hereby disclaims any responsibility for them.

Inks and Bindings
888-290-5218
www.inksandbindings.com
orders@inksandbindings.com

Contents

Chapter 1
OLD MEXICO WHITETAIL HUNT

DAY ONE

Out and about, we're on our way across the border for hopefully a big whitetail deer. We left Louisiana December 26 right after a good Christmas, celebrating the birth of our Lord and Savior Jesus Christ. We ended up staying in the Holiday Inn in Zapata, Texas.

DAY TWO

Up and on our way down to Falcon Heights to meet our party to cross the border with. We drove around a bit to find permission and a safe place to leave my Toyota truck. My insurance would only cover my vehicle twenty miles in so I decided it would be best not to take it across border. We headed to hunt in Paras Nuevo Leon, a town established in February of 1851. It was a prior settlement of the Guleno Indians. This makes it a bit more exciting because Tiffany and I love artifact hunting. The area is known for artifacts as well but a big whitetail is our main goal. All we need is a passport or birth certificate to pass through the border. Going across the border was no issue at all but they knew Scott, our outfitter, well. They didn't even look at our passports or anything. So, pretty much, no one even knew we were here. About thirty minutes later, we were on the ranch. We were staying at what looked to be an old farm house, guessing to be built around the 50's.

Pretty quickly, we headed out to a nice double box blind. The weather was damp, misting rain, windy and cool. Not long after a few feathered friends flew by, deer and javelina popped out in all directions. Over a dozen does, four or five bucks with spreads just out to the ears but no shooters. Right at dark, coyotes busted loose with their cries gathering to prepare for a hunt.

Back at camp, we spent the first night by a nice fire, to try to keep warm while waiting for baked potatoes cooking in coals and some ribeye's as well. The first night was cool and comfortable and pretty quiet.

DAY THREE

Up at daylight getting dressed fast because there wasn't any heat. I was glad another hunter had brewed up a good pot of swamp water, even with no sugar to be found, it was a welcoming taste. Soon we was loaded and trucking, after I scarfed down a bear claw for breakfast.

Morning in the stand was great and full of action. There was about seven bucks in all with one pushing about 120 inches. He was trying to hold a doe by keeping other bucks fought back. Tiffany was trying hard to get some good pictures of local birds, while keeping an eye out for a shooter. It was cool to watch a few quail with binos too. Action slowed, but there were always deer passing every fifteen or twenty minutes right up until we left at about 11:15 a.m.

After a fast lunch and a quick nap, we were back in the stand for the evening hunt. Just an hour into it, we had twenty-seven does at one time and one fourteen-inch eight point. It was a bit warmer evening than yesterday. At about 500 yards, we had two big hogs cross. On the way in, we hit a wash out and had a good bit of corn spill out. This was undoubtedly where those hogs were headed. Later, three bucks came out. One was a cull buck but really never gave us a good shot. It wasn't long after that that five javelina came out. One had two babies about the size of my fists that made for a bit of entertainment. We had used the range finder earlier in case some javelina came out, so Tiffany could try to take one with a crossbow. Sure enough one, without little ones, came out right in front of the box stand. Tiffany had to slide over to make the shot and did. Bad deal was the limb hit the edge of the window. The arrow bounced and it sounded like someone hit the box stand with a 2x4. The string popped off and javelina and deer went everywhere. Unfortunately, there was no way of restoring it without a press. So, it made for a bad evening. Just at dark, one of the guys shot and sounded like a hit on a big pig, probably a boar. We all tried to find it with no luck. Then, to put the icing on the cake, I realized that I had left my 30.06 leaning up by the stand, so we had to go back and get it. Not a great day, so I was happy to close my lids and hope for a better tomorrow.

DAY FOUR

Out and in the stand plenty of time before daylight. It was a cool morning, misty with overcast. Even before day break, I could barely see the white of a deer's butt. Eventually, we had about nine or eleven deer feeding on corn that we had put out before daylight, with a buddy feeder, attached to the receiver hitch, of a pickup truck. Soon followed a lot of quail and cottontails to help pass the time of the morning hunt. Like most hunts, we heard the coyotes howling at the morning sun. We had this one particularly dark doe that acted as if it had never seen a person. She stayed within ten yards of us, giving us an amazing viewing of her beauty. Finally, two bucks came out, one eight point and one six point. Still no shooters. Crap!

Back to camp we got a good fire started and then moved the firewood under the roof to keep it dry. We cleaned up a bit then ate a big breakfast burrito. Since, we had to go to town to get more ice and air up a tire, we decided to hunt a thousand-acre ranch they had close by.

There was no stands set up yet so we brought some little folding chairs and shooting sticks. We found a place to set up, but me and Tiff decided it was a good place and time and weather to stalk a bit. So, I cranked the Nikon scope down to three power and off we went, slowly following the heaviest trails we could find. Most of the time though, thirty yards was as far as we could see in every direction. We ran into a few scrapes on the ground, which answered one Alabama boy's question of, if they even do that down here having so many does. Yes they do! My worry was that Tiff would not be paying attention, looking for arrow heads, when I see something and stop. Thank God that didn't happen because the Lord sent me slap dab on top of my first big Mexico Whitetail buck, bedded just twenty yards in front of me. All I could see were some horns and a neck, so I knew what to do. Well duh, shoot him in the neck, so I did. Dead in his tracks! Stoked as I could be at the way it all went down, I am feeling so blessed to be in all God's glory in this cactus country of old Mexico.

The deer was thick necked with a real black face and chocolate horns, it was all I had wished for. No complaints for sure. Waiting on Scott to pick us up, we sat along the old road and seen a fine four point later. Who knows it might be the buck in four years from now that I cross paths with, if the good Lord wills me another day for another hunt. I'm always thankful first for the deer. We ended the day with quail and mallard duck for supper.

DAY FIVE

We got to the stand in plenty of time this morning with the action starting a little later than usual. The does seemed to be a little less tolerant of each other and a few, I could tell was trying to nudge their babies off. Soon we saw some nice bucks but none were shooters. We were praying one was a cull buck though. We got some nice pics and a couple of videos. Two javelina crept up on us as well as a real pretty, whiter than normal doe. I called in a coyote but missed it crossing the road. I forgot that the gun, I'm using, has a hair pin trigger.

So about 9:40, we decided to stalk a bit. About a mile and a half into it, along a long fence line, we spotted a very nice buck. We decided to pass on it and take a video instead, it was tough. Unfortunately, he was too big for a cull buck and too small for a trophy. It was awesome to have laid eyes on him anyways. At about the time we saw Scott coming to get us, we spotted two hogs so I tried a 450-yard shot, with his 30.06 but no luck.

For the evening hunt, we made the thirty-minute drive back to the 1000-acre ranch. Two does were out a good while. One was really black and seemed not to be able to hold her ears up and looked mad all the time. About thirty minutes before dark, I had noticed the single doe we had out kept looking back. Then I saw him at about 200 yards, one of the two things I still hope to take before I leave this world. A huge six point! By the time I was sure, all I could see was head, horns, his butt and tail. He was behind some bushes working a scrape. After about five minutes, he just disappeared. So, I waited five minutes hoping he'd step out but he did not. So, I threw out a snort wheeze call and a few grunts. Nothing. About now, I'm hanging my head. Ten minutes later he's back out farther down. Now, I had to be sure not to shoot the wrong one. Yelp, it was him. Now, I'm on the ground with no rest, in a dang lawn chair, and felt buck fever with a surprise because I haven't had that in a while. Well, I done my best and squeezed the trigger. Five minutes later, with daylight falling fast, we went down to see if we could find blood. Crap! None to be seen. So, the old sick disgusted feeling with a lot of Damns, come out. I started to look in the thick for him and then low and behold I saw a buck and again I had to be sure. By the time I was sure he was darting off and I took a shot, but shouldn't have. He ran a good ways, tail bobbing and again he was gone. This was one of those dang times I'd have to suck it up and lick my wounds and get over it. We did end up catching a nice size tarantula spider and seen a blue indigo snake, which are pretty rare. Big suckers too. Roast beef filled our bellies before hitting the hay.

DAY SIX

We started this day in the coon stand. A lot of does and management bucks fed around us this morning. My plan was to wipe out some javelinas but after taking four down, I realized I had only brought six bullets. Damn! Well that ended that mission. I don't want to be out if a big buck happens to pass my way. Our outfitter, Scott, had planned to leave for Houston and return January 2, 2018. Today is New Year's Eve. Since, he planned to pull out by noon, we figured he'd be picking us up around nine or ten. Well one o' clock rolls around and still no Scott. Hmm…we had started to think something terrible had happened. Surely, we weren't supposed to stay out all night without any arrangements. We decided we would start walking at three o' clock. It would have been about a three-and-a-half-hour walk. So, around two o'clock, I decided to take a walk around our stand, while Tiffany stayed behind and looked for arrowheads. About thirty minutes later, here come the other two hunters, Bill and Jeff in their truck. We thought Scott had already left for the border and they were here to pick us up. They seemed surprised and asked Tiffany what stand Scott had dropped us off at. She replied, "Um, here." Bill told her Scott had been looking for us for hours. The only reason they were even driving by was because Jeff had forgotten his jacket in a blind further down the road, dubbed the Hakuna Matata stand. Thankfully God was on our side that day! We laughed about it on the way back to the ranch and I had to give Scott a rough time about it.

With Scott gone a few days, we were on our own, so I decided to get his Kawasaki mule ready to go. I filled the tank and fashioned a tarp over the top to give us some protection from the upcoming rain. I was leery about the passenger back tire right from the get go. Loaded up a few chairs and we were gone to check some new places out. It became clear that we weren't going very far in this relic. Finding a spot to try, I spread corn and then parked. I made sure the key was turned off because I've been down that road before. Just to my right, a buck popped out at the end of the trail. The more I looked at him, the more I liked him. He was about 225 yards.

TIFFANY

I was sitting there listening to Ch talk about a buck that he was seeing in the binos. I thought he looked good as well and figured he was contemplating on taking him. He was concerned about taking a long shot with a rifle that was not his own. It was supplied by the ranch. So, I blurt out that he should go sneak up on him. I knew he was capable and also enjoyed the thrill of it. Finally, he said ok and told me to run to the first bush closest me when he said go and then wait to follow him when he got there. I was pumped up for a little excitement. Then completely unexpectedly he hands me the gun. Shocked, I asked him" aren't you going to need this to shoot him?" He said," you're going to shoot him!" Now I'm a bundle of nerves and weakly asked, "I am?"

"Go now!" he snaps. With no time to argue, I run to the spot he pointed out a moment ago, with him following quickly behind. He takes the lead at his stealthy yet swift pace. In all honesty, I'm not very good at it. I can do fast or quiet, but not both at the same time. My heart is pounding and I'm breathing hard from adrenaline as we follow the brush closer and closer to the buck. Ch turns to me and tells me to calm down. I tell him I'll try but, my body denies his request. At thirty yards, hidden behind a cactus, we are looking at him head on. I'm worried now, because I've only shot one deer and I'm uncomfortable with a neck shot. Ch breaks some twigs from in front of my barrel. He must have told me like five times to shoot but I just couldn't get my hands and arms to steady my gun. Finally, I shoot. Before I know it, Ch grabs the gun and shoots again dropping him in his tracks. At first, I thought I had missed but he explained that he wanted to make sure the buck didn't run off into all the cactus around. Which is completely understandable.

Even though, he wasn't a great big buck, it was definitely a great buck for me, since we had successfully stalked it together. We pulled it to the shade and went back to see if Ch's dream buck would make an appearance. Unfortunately, no dream buck, only a very spooky doe and little buck. With a light rain coming down on us, we decided to end the hunt. So, we hop in the rig to go pick up me deer but it wouldn't start. Also, the tire Ch had warned Scott about... yep, it was flat. Crud! We knew Jeff wouldn't want to take his truck down on that rough road and we certainly were not going to ask him either. Wondering how we were going to get this deer out of here, I saw the tarp and suggested we use it to tote the deer to camp. He told me to grab it and then he went to work.

Watching Ch dissemble the deer, I am truly amazed and impressed on how skillfully he field dresses the deer. Gutting and deboning the animal and diligently cutting it into pieces so that we could take as much meat as possible. Neither of us could stand the thought of wasting any of it and I was thanking God for the take and prayed that He approved. After watching Ch, I gained even more love and respect for him this night. We each took an end of the now heavy tarp and started toward the road. Once we got to the road, we dropped the tarp and walked on in to camp. Jeff didn't mind picking up the meat off the main road for us at all. Back at camp Ch quickly finished piecing my deer and putting it on ice. First though, he skinned out Bill's boar snout that he had taken earlier. It took him like a whole two minutes! Wow! With a long fruitful day in the books, we scarfed done some sandwiches and went to bed.

DAY SEVEN
VICTOR

Out the door with a pastry, we went to the green stand, they call it. But weather had dropped out from under us that night, getting to butt cold fast at about 25 degrees. So this stand didn't have any windows to stop the wind and we had sleet, snow and rain off and on for three hours, blowing sideways like a bird in a hurricane. It was the first time my 1200-gram Lacrosse boots left my feet chilly. Fo sho! We saw a good many deer, quail and cara all wanting a bite of the corn we had put out. One good 130-inch buck and some smaller bucks were chasing one ole doe hoping she'd give into a little love.

We came back in to camp about 11 a.m. and practically threw ourselves into the fire to warm up. I even took three nips out of my moonshine bottle. I only drink it to help keep the cold off best I can. That evening we headed to what they call the coon stand. It's a nice double box stand with windows. The strong wind still had them rattling from every direction. To prevent the windows from fogging up too bad, we put and empty shell casing under one window.

It didn't take too long before we wished we had brought our little buddy heater. We saw a lot of deer moving about. There were about six bucks, some cull, and some management. But then, the biggest body deer I had seen yet, with a hard to pass set of antlers for sure came in our view. Anyway, I shot him with the camera and videoed him with my phone. Which isn't always a bad thing but I think I messed up because his big body, I fear, made his antlers look smaller than they actually were.

It was definitely one of those nights, after a hunt, that I couldn't wait to see the headlights coming in the dark and feel the warmth of the heater in the truck. You should always, though, have what you need in case you have to make a cold night out. Quick meal with leftover steak and potatoes before we tried to murder the bed to sleep.

DAY EIGHT

It was still colder than being on Pike's Peak in your underwear when we woke up this morning. We slept in this morning with the moon being full. Some new hunters had come in from Atlanta and Pennsylvania to shoot footage for their You Tube show. We stoked the fire up and finished a cup of coffee and headed out. Pretty quick, deer started passing by us every now and then. Some blue quail and a few javelina came by, with their babies and one crippled one with a club foot. Also, a few great up and comer bucks that we haven't seen before were out. Then like deer do, like a ghost, a perfect main frame twelve-point steps out. Now, I knew that twelve points, or anything close, with a near perfect rack is rare. Of course, my window was down so I had to ease it up slowly and as quietly as I could, all the while my heart was pounding in my chest. To make matters tenser, there were three or four does at spitting distance from me. So, I waited patiently, for a good dead in his tracks shot to the neck and done just that at about 50 yards. So now rested another lifelong dream, in the welcome sunlight, of a simple man. Ole Southern boy was happy from one end to the other right there.

So, we went down to show honor and praise to the beautiful majestic beast and pray over his body for food that he will provide me and friends in sharing the blessing. After taking a few photos, we got him gutted and moved to shade. Then we propped his carcass open, toward the cool wind, until we were picked up. No meat hardly wasted by this ole boy. To do so with me is stealing from Nature and God. So, if you don't have someone that will eat the meat or yourself, then don't shoot it. Now, some animals are different, of course, such as those animals that can harm more wildlife and the environment such as wild hogs and the javelina here, in the big cactus thickets, of Old Mexico.

DAY NINE
TIFFANY

Scott came by and scooped up Ch's twelve point. He was happy. He had two other hunters with him, Brandon and Joe. Joe has also killed a very nice eight point. Scott brought us burritos and gorditas and something to wash it all down with, so we could stay the duration of the day. We didn't see a whole lot more deer, just a few does and small bucks but then Ch spotted a big hog cross the road at around 1220 yards from us. He'd been seeing them cross there a few times already.

He said, "We ought to go stalk that bastard." I was reluctant. "There goes another one," he said with excitement in his voice, which I've learned means he wants it. In this case he wanted it for me. He truly enjoys the vicarious thrill when someone takes an animal that he has helped them stalk. We trekked down the road and it wasn't too long before we found where the boar had cut in to some brush. Ch spotted him quickly at about 150 yards out. He kneeled down and put the rifle on his left shoulder, for me to use as a rest. I cannot seem to stay steady. Not as near crazy nervous I was yesterday when I shot the eight point but still shaky. I wanted him down with no discrepancy this time. Seeing an animal suffer is sickening to me so I sure didn't want to be the cause of it. With all of this stirring in my mind, I decided a head shot would be the best option. In my scope, out of my scope, in, out. Oh why cannot I not stop shaking? Deep breath and boom. Thank God, he was down where he stood! Ch was happy, which always makes me happy. After a high five, we went to check out the boar. Ch was very surprised by the size of his cutters. I really had no idea what a good size was so I thought he was just trying to build me up even more. Bony and kind of decrepit, it was apparent this boar was a pretty old guy, now shrunken with age, as we all do.

So, what do we do now? Well, that first bigger boar, is still out there and you can bet Ch is chomping at the bit at a chance for him. Ch took off like a leopard with me lagging behind, which he scolded me for. We stopped and I thought the hunt was over, with the sun making its descent behind, us but Ch spotted him and lit out again. We were approximately 225 yards, when Ch got a glimpse of the hog. Since he really loves stalking and getting as close as possible to the prey, we crept closer. All of a sudden, he comes to a dead stop and boom. In a blink of an eye Ch took off after the boar leaving me in the dust. He took a shot but unfortunately, he missed him. We did look for about ten or fifteen minutes to make sure it was a miss but without seeing any blood and darkness setting in and no headlights, we decided it was a miss. Quickly, we made our way back to my boar where Ch methodically removed the head from the body. I grabbed my hog head and we fast tracked it back to the stand to wait for pickup. When we got back to camp, Ch realized that he had turned his scope up to eight for me and forgotten to turn it back down. This was probably the reason he missed his boar. Too bad because he really wanted a double take on boars.

The three other hunters had all taken animals that day as well. So, everyone was busy cutting or skinning something. I sawed my snout off all by myself. Probably not a big deal for most people but I was a little proud. Cutting through teeth is not easy. I had almost finished fleshing it out when Ch took over. He's so much faster than I am, he had already caped out his own twelve point. I think we can both agree that it was an awesome day for both of us. It was also an exceptional day for Brandon too. He killed the best buck of his life, a bobcat and a sow!

We are all sleeping on success tonight.

DAY TEN

This morning we decided to go arrow head hunting and fishing after drinking a cup of coffee. We found a few chips but nothing too exciting. Fishing ended up pretty much the same way. After eating, we headed to the other ranch at about 1:30. The weather is so crazy. This morning we woke up to a frigid 35 degrees and now its 65 degrees! While driving, we spotted a Blue Indigo snake about seven foot long, crossing the road. I bailed out and caught him or her and could easily see why they were given their name. They are a beautiful blue translucent color. I let him go with a kiss since they eat rattlesnakes. The drive was a bit rough with four people sitting in the back of the truck. We stopped by the local store to set up a plan to donate meat from the hunts to the locals, especially from the guys that fly instead of drive. It's got where it is very expensive to bring back meat. I don't see PETA folks feeding thousands of animals or donating any food. We, the hunters, feed millions of birds, raccoons, squirrels, even predators and rodents, while deer hunting, because of all the corn and food plots we provide. During this time of year animals need the extra food the most. Along with this, it makes the value of corn and stuff well worth growing to help farmers help folks and eat in the process.

At the ranch, we plop down in our chairs. We kind of cut some limbs for a makeshift blind and settled in for five hours. It wasn't long before we had some entertainment from some chubby quail and some other colorful birds that made for some nice pictures. The temps had heated up quite a bit. Sitting there and dozing, a couple of does pop out. It wasn't until darn near dark until we saw a nice 120 inch or so buck, a three point and a four point. Also, one doe that was a bit in heat because big boy was on her, off and on, grunting the whole time. Downhill the boys from Pursuit T.V., had been shooting all evening. They took some haveys, a couple of pigs and ended up with a great tall, 147-inch eight point and a 125 or so inch nine point.

Back at the camp, we grilled some pink meat from the bobcat they had shot earlier. We concluded it was pretty darn good, actually. Everyone gathered outside looking over the deer and telling stories.

DAY ELEVEN

We got up later than planned, since I lost sleep because of the ranch dog, Pinta. Good dog, but she gets right by the window and barks throughout the night at the yelping coyotes. We decided to do a camp clean up. So, we started off by sweeping off the porches and picking up cans and trash. Then, we rearranged a few things, fixed the feeder that goes on the truck and unclogged the toilet and cleaned it up a bit. Then coffee and back out to the coon stand, that ought to be named the Doe stand!

We weren't there long before a bunch of does, javeys and a few bucks showed up. There was one good buck that showed up that made me think twice but I took some pics and videos and let him walk. There is about a 500-acre block no one has hunted in, next to the coon stand so we decided to scout it a bit. While walking it, we spotted a three-acre pond. In the pond was a good many ducks. Man, it was killing me wanting to hunt them. All the while, we were looking for arrow heads, searching for main deer trails, crossings, pinch points and possible stand sites. I climbed the windmill that we came across, to get a better look. At the other end there was about a ten-acre lake with a real good flock of pelicans mixed with ducks on it. We made them fly for a chance at some good pictures. It took a while to walk through and around it.

Back in the stand, we kicked off our boots and got down to t-shirts. It's crazy considering that we couldn't get warm for anything a few days ago all day long. I then laid my head down for a bit. When I raised up, I saw a bobcat walking away from us down the road about 220 yards and tried to take a pop shot. I'm not sure if I missed or not. It wasn't long before a nice 80 inch up and comer, came out behind us about 2:15 p.m. After that, an eight point came out, that we had seen many times. We named him Old Boy, because his horns were well on their way down and what many would consider a cull buck on a management ranch. Of course there wasn't any shortage of quail and doves flurrying about now and then and as always plenty of does as well.

Back at the ranch we packed up to head back home. I wasn't quite ready to leave but work was calling as it always does. My plan was to wrap things up quickly at home and recruit a few friends to join me in sharing this awesome wild country that held so much wild life. If all goes well, I'll be back in a couple of weeks. So long for now Mexico! As always we are so very thankful to live and have the opportunity to revel in God's amazing creation.

Chapter 2
SECOND TRIP TO MEXICO
WIDE BUCK

January 20, 2018

So. 5 a.m. sharp, Robert, Jeff, Mike and I lit out for the long drive back across the border. I ended up making the whole trip driving. Of course, I had to talk their heads off with old stories and a cup of coffee now and then, to stay awake. It wasn't hard to see that we were going hunting with a truck load of hunting stuff in the back. At the border, they rummaged through our things but no too bad. This was the first time I had ever drove my own truck across. Having the registration and insurance was the main thing I needed. Not sure, but with confidence, we found our way down the highways to Paras. But we did have a bit of trouble finding the ranch road. We still managed to make it in at about 9 p.m., even after setting up a ground blind, for me, on the other ranch.

DAY 1

Up and out of bed, we lit out to some stands being about half sure we were even headed the right way. After getting Jeff and Robert set up, me and Mike climbed in the coon box stand together. It was fast to see deer and ended up seeing nineteen does and five bucks at one time. No real shooters though. We had hoped to see a cull buck Tiffany and I called Old Boy, for Mike to take. He never showed. Jeff took his first javelina and Robert had a ball seeing all of the deer, including a wide four point. We have not yet made our minds up on if it was a cull or not. Cull bucks are those you don't want breeding does in the herd. It's just not great genetics like small antlers on three-year-olds or older, and having two antlers on one side and five on the other etc.

For the evening hunt, we all went to the High 6 Ranch, I call it, the thousand-acre ranch. Me and Robert were in my ground blind. Jeff was on the tripod and Mike was at the Red Hill stand. Me and Robert saw a big buck late, too late unfortunately, to be one hundred percent sure that it was a shooter. The bad part was that we had gotten the time all wrong and this morning we got to the stand way too early, waiting on daylight.

DAY 2

Up at the right time this morning, we gulped some badly needed coffee down and went to drop Robert off and did. Then one mile away we figured out he had gotten the wrong box of shells. Not good. So we turned around and headed his way. Then we rode through the world and back trying to find the darn Hog Stand, they call it. But with having no luck, Jeff and I ended up just setting up lawn chairs at an intersection in the road. About thirty minutes or so later, we about had a young doe get in the chairs with us. Later, two more came out on the roadside nibbling at this and that along the road's edge. They would disappear and then show up again. A roadrunner buzzed by and a nice nine-point buck, about 120 inches, popped out. Beautiful deer. We sat a bit longer and decided to stalk this javey up the road, with no luck. So, we lit out for a hike through the prickly pear cactus. Then suddenly, a jack rabbit ran out from under a pile of limbs and stopped about twenty yards. Jeff flung an arrow at it but had no luck with a hit. We finished out the hunt with some scouting and headed in.

The evening hunt started after a nice nap. Jeff and I headed down the rough rock road to the coon stand, a two-person box blind. We dropped Mike off in a spot in a swag where it is thick on each side of the road with a lake on each side. I had seen a few large hog tracks in that area and Mike had never taken a hog. He hoped to get a good boar. Low and behold, he did. Dropped him right in the road. He said it was just lying there. So he set his gun down and climbed out of his little chair blind. But when he got out it was gone! Oops! Never found him. We looked but had no luck.

Jeff and I had deer on us pretty quick but in the middle of it we got down and stalked javelinas. Both of us ended up with two each with his bow and got them all on video. It was a lot of fun. Those things sound like a wood pecker pecking a tree when they're slapping their jaws.

Back in the stand hoping to see the wise cull buck, Old Boy. The stars must have been lined up right because soon as the wind died down, he appeared like a ghost, right behind us. Jeff shot and missed. Out the stand we went. While looking for it we saw him cross another road. Jeff shot again and up the hill he ran and got another shot, his third shot. No luck at all. We both had a pissed and disgusted feeling thinking the gun must be off. Robert had shot a javelina on the first day with it and had put it on nine power and we didn't know it. We think that had something to do with it. So, now back in the stand again, just hoping to see maybe a hog when, shockingly, Old Boy came out again, in front of us, at eighty yards. This time Jeff gave him a dirt nap, in the shoulder, turning a frustrating evening into a happy one.

DAY 3

This morning me and Mike headed fifteen miles to High 6 ranch on the other side of Paras. I climbed into my stand and had one heck of a show with all the colorful birds, doves and quail. The wind made it pretty chilly. Eventually, two does popped out, at right about 200 yards, down along with about a seventeen-inch eight point, but that was about it. We did have five javelina come out a good ways down the lane. After seeing they were not gonna feed our way, we decided to make a stalk for Mike's first cross bow kill for one of these rodents that stink to hell and back. They are interesting critters with big teeth that pop like the sound that a wood pecker makes on a tree. They can be eaten when cleaned and cooked the right way. I ate my first one in Sonora, Mexico. So on the stalk, it didn't take me long to see Mike's noisy boots weren't made for walking. Eventually, he ended up putting them in sticker bushes he calls prickly pear. Good part was we ended up spotting one on the edge of the road and Mike popped it while I videoed it. It wasn't quite dead but he didn't plan to go in after it having fear he would get eaten up. Probably was a good reason. Luckily, he could see it and was close enough to finish it off quickly so not to let it suffer and help out some starving coyotes and buzzards.

The evening hunt was slow although we all saw some nice deer including an eight point up and comer that I saw.

DAY 4

We were back on Armando's 5000-acre ranch, the Violin. We all headed to stands with corn that we finally picked up in Paras. This corn is different from what I am used to at home. It has a strong sweet popcorn kinda smell that I believe allows the deer to wind, from hundreds of yards away. I have no idea what they add to it. I ended up on what I call the cultipacker stand. There is about a forty-acre area that had been cleaned over. I opened the spreader feeder on the truck and corned the road in front of me. I'd never hunted here so I didn't know what to expect but with plenty of deer tracks around it, I knew it couldn't be too awful a bad of spot.

It wasn't too long before two does popped out then three more. They fed for about twenty minutes when a nice nine point stepped out with a cull four point. That was about right, he couldn't have popped out for Robert who was looking for a cull. I climbed out of the stand to make a little walk and scout some also and came upon about a five-acre lake. Working my way around the edge trying to stick to cover and move slow and quiet, I spotted a hog about 400 yards. I made my way to about 225 yards and laid my barrel in the form of a small dead tree for a rest. Turned my scope up a bit, held my breath and squeezed the trigger. Sha zoom boom! Hit but it darted into brush like a bat out of hell. Finally making my way through the muck, I got to where I thought it had to be and then it busted out of the tall grass. I shot again and downed it. I don't know if it just was running because it heard or smelled me or was charging. Either way I did not take any chances. It ended up being a red rust colored sow about 180 pounds.

Getting back to the ranch, everyone had seen game and Mike got a shot at a bobcat crossing a road, with a miss. We ended the evening hunt all seeing game. I think Mike saw the biggest buck in his life though. Seeing a lot of ducks in the pond had me scratching for a good duck hunt. The weather has cooled to about 40 degrees at night and 60 degrees in the day, so not too shabby to hunt in if you can keep out of the blazing sun.

DAY 5

Woke up 5:15, to cool temps, hot coffee and then scarfed down a couple of muffins and was ready to roll out. I ended up hunting the stand I call Jacked Black because someone did not center the ladder to the door. I had a ball watching eleven does and five bucks. They were all temperamental about another deer eating too close to them and a few fought a good bit. Too funny! There was one nice ten point about 135 inches. It was hard to pass on that. After rounding up the guys, we headed in quickly to the cook shack to devour some gumbo and crackers like a pack of starving marvins.

I left out at about noon headed to the H6 ranch. Getting there, I decided to do a bit of work prepping for next season, by trimming some limbs back that was trying to drag all the paint off the sides of my truck. Climbed in my double bull blind and it wasn't long before I got a little rain. Quickly I was in a fight to keep my head from dropping off my neck. About got whiplash several times trying to stay awake. From the long lane to my right a doe popped out and there was two javelinas in front. I had seen a big fresh hog track walking in and my trail camera confirmed it was a good one so I hoped to see it, as well. Had a pleasure watching and videoing some birds that I haven't seen yet. One kind of looked like a roadrunner but it wasn't. Temps dropped a bit then I saw just a neck and head sticking out of the edge of the lane. It was a buck. Eyes glued to the binos, I could see fairly quickly that it was no giant but obvious it was a cull buck. So one step more from ole boy and I was gonna send a bullet sailing from about 186 yards in his direction and did, smack down in his tracks! He had mismatched antlers with seven total points.

Now, getting dark and the rain getting harder, so I eased out of my blind. Of course a doe steps out and busts me. I put on my slicker suit and gutted the deer. I figured this would be my last hunt on the H6 this season, so I broke down my double bull blind, tossed away the limbs beside it, packed it up and headed to the truck. Now all alone, I had a ball with mud on my boots, getting this buck loaded up in the back of my Toyota, with a four-inch lift kit, but managed.

DAY 6

Misting rain and cool temps at about 40 degrees, we lit out. I ended up seeing about twenty-eight deer, two bucks. They were good up and comers but not shooters. Then there was a heck of a fight between to male javelinas that lasted about twenty minutes. Jaws just a snapping the whole time. One ended up walking on three legs. It's funny how they scratch each other's butts. They have a scent gland located on their rump so I gather that must be some of the reason.

DAY 7

This evening we decided just to clean up and pack down camp to get ready for the next day to drive home and cross the border at Falcon Lake. We did cross without any troubles thanks to God. This was around the time that El Chapo had recently been caught so it was the beginning of allot of unrest for the country that could have so much to offer with true frontier for hunting if it weren't for the drugs. I'm blessed to have visited there. There had been some hairy times there off and on but reality is that there is more crime in every town in the USA, a month than some the towns across border in a year. But when the cartels involved it's usually bad. It is usually best just to stay off roads at night and out sight as much as you can.

Chapter 3
HOG HUNT SIMPSON WMA 2017

This little hunt came from about three months of scouting and hiking on what is now part of Peason Ridge WMA, in Vernon Parish Louisiana. This land is part of the second time the government took land to expand the Ft. Polk training area. Some of the houses that were taken, were only two months old. I think it was a lot of infrastructure they wanted. A lot of the land was from timber companies. On these hikes, I kept crossing paths with tracks of a large hog, the print was as big as the palm of my hand, some even bigger. With the season not yet open, I didn't pursue it too much but started to see that he seemed to stay within a two-mile area.

Now in this area, was the last man standing, I call him, yet to be shoved out, Mr. Lewis. He was born on the twenty acres there in 1949, land that his grandpa had bought. Now older, most of it had pasture that had grown into large thickets. On the edge was a stock pond with water all up in it and full of hog sign. I figured a lot of them summered in this thicket because of the water. In the thicket, there was a spring fed creek winding its way through along with spots where hogs had wallowed in the mud old and new. You could smell them in some places also. A lot of tracks mixed with a few deer tracks too. Archery season was now open, so I decided to give it a try in there. So, I marked me a trail in and attached a climber to a tree about 40 minutes before daylight. The little stock pond was about 500 yards away. Now about 25 feet high, jacked up in a pine tree, it didn't take long to whip out the thermocell for mosquitos. It was bearable but enough to annoy any man. Warm and muggy, with temps most won't even think about hunting in. Morning breezed by, and had heated up. So about 9:30 a.m. I came down and headed out to mark a tree and cut a trail through a thicket, in a clear cut, to one lone pine tree out there, preparing for a possible gun hunt there later.

DAY 2

I was out early after some toast and coffee. The morning was a bit cooler. After listening to a few hoot owls talking around me, a glimmer of daylight had broken out. Soon, I heard faint grunts in the background with an occasional snort or blow. At about 100 yards a big black blob coming right to me. Easing my bow off the rest of my climber, I clicked my release on. It stopped now and then but kept coming. Soon, it was about ten yards from the base of the tree that I was in, right under me! I drew my bow. Darn, still so dark that I could not see my sight through my peep. Not Good. So, I instinctively shot for the back and it was a hard hit. Thump! It squealed and tore through the thicket in front of me. From the sounds of it, it stopped about 100 yards and all I heard for about fifteen minutes were sounds like it was dying, with grunts now and then. I knew not to jump down and push it too fast, like with most anything that doesn't drop in its tracks when it has been hit with an arrow. I planned to sit for at least one and half hours. Judging by the size, I truly felt that I must have gotten into the big hog that I had been tracking. I assumed it was a boar or a bar hog. A bar hog is a boar that has been caught with dogs, cut and then released back. It wasn't about a half hour later that I heard hogs fighting, probably over acorns. Soon I was in bow range, about 35 yards. After ten minutes or so of being patient, I got on a perfect size sow, about 100 pounds. I drew my bow and slung the 100 grain broad head through her and she wheeled and squealed for about thirty yards and then piled up. Some of the others ran to her so I pulled another arrow and slung it into another one and it ran straight into the thicket. They just kept coming but I ran out of arrows. About 30 minutes later, I came down and found two of my arrows. I started to track the first, and what I hoped to be a monster hog. Going into the thicket to where I had to crawl a few times wasn't good if I was to meet up with a wounded hog. All I had was a four-inch knife. Well, it wasn't looking good fast. Tracks were in every direction and no blood to follow. Man. I was kinda sick. This would have been a giant. But it's not the first one to get away and probably won't be the last. With the heat rising, I had to move the sow as not to chance spoiling a good sow. I chose eating over a skull to put on the wall. Dragging her out was for the birds. So I called Mr. Lewis and I went up the road to his place to cool her down with a water hose. We skinned her and I gave him half. So at least some pork, from the last hog taken, in the old place, went to the last man standing on it. Get out there! Can't wait on the weather always. You never know what kind of day God may give yea until you go.

Chapter 4
COON HUNTING

W ow Coon hunting! There can't be a better way to spend a night in the woods than chasing ole ridge running a coon with an ole blue tick or red bone hound or any dog, with or without a great friend. Some of the best times I had as a young boy was with my dogs at night, with a light looking up a tree trying to spot a set of eyes or a few sets. It's good to watch yea dog work a trail an ole coon has traveled along a creek bank, through ole swamp, giving a bark now and then before he ends up treeing. There's a whole other world at night.

One story I like to tell is one with an ole friend that is not in this world now. A friend that I spent many nights chasing coons and opossums, AZ Corley. Now one night, and a school night at that, we started out at Big Ben Creek, we called it, with a good chance of rain. Soon we were out and moving our way along the creek through small swamps, flooded timber with cypress knees that looked like monsters. We were just waiting for AZ's dog, Hobo and my Blue tick, Blueboy, to strike. Hobo was a cur pit mix and could out hunt many a Grand Nite champion and he did. But since he didn't have any papers and his daddy was picked up at a local trash dump and would sometimes tree an opossum, we could not enter him in the competition. It wasn't too long before the bottom fell out and we were soaked. Nevertheless, the dogs went trailing and after crossing a few logs and jumping some brush we caught up to them. About that time they had treed and Hobo was up to his signature flip off the tree already and Blueboy was loping around the tree spilling a long howling cry now and then followed up by three or four fast barks that kinda sounded like it was killing him. With our elastic head bands with six-volt batteries, we were looking up a beech tree full of holes and vines. We couldn't afford high dollar coon lights back then. We couldn't see anything and figured it was in a hole so like flushing a squirrel out, we built a small fire at the bottom of the tree and made it smoke bad. About ten minutes later, sure enough two coons lit out of the tree to higher ground, in a big pine close by. Coon's hides would fetch twelve to twenty-two dollars each so we sent a .22 long rifle bullet through them. Then, after a huge thump when the coons hit the ground, the dogs had their satisfaction gnawing on them a bit before we tied them and tossed them over our backs and lit out again. Later, we heard Hobo vaguely up the creek and had to hunt him up. When we did he was darn near all the way in a hole in the ground that would make a badger look like an amateur. Digging after what we assumed was an opossum. He didn't fool with armadillos much. What happened next is why I remember this story over so many others. AZ ended up in the hole now with nothing more than his legs out trying to get the opossum out and actually done it without being bitten. When he slung it out, of course the dogs ganged up on it and killed it. Now lights dimmer and time passing. We kinda pushing the time that our parents preferred us to be home. But them knowing the boys we were, they knew it was nothing unusual for us to be later than earlier. It was cool like that and never a problem unless grades dropped.

The next time they treed, we ended up going through a few thickets to a pine plantation that had a strand of hardwood that ran through it. Shining for this coon we realized our night needed to end soon because lights were dimming enough that we weren't going to find this coon. So after many steps later, we finally made our way back to the creek. So tired of dragging these dang coons through brush, we decided to stop and go ahead and skin them to lighten the load. While we were skinning them, what charge was left in my battery was drained and my light went out. About this time a curious owl watching let out a scream, at what seemed ten feet away and it scared AZ enough that he dropped his light causing his bulb to bust! Not good. Now in the dark, real dark, we started making our way home as fast as we could. Now for me it wasn't great but not really bad, but for AZ, well he wore coke bottle glasses, we called them back then. I tell yea, when we got out of them woods and hit Hwy 111, for about a three mile walk back to the three-wheeler, there was no doubt that the only thing we cared about was a bed.

At fifty now, I remember bits and pieces of many of my hunts but most of this one has never faded. The bond of boys and their dogs, while hunting, can be one of true love in its own way. Every boy needs a best friend growing up. Having a dog to feed and fetch a ball is one thing but spending time in the woods together is of a different way. I thank God all of the time that I grew up the way I did and that my best friend was not a damn cell phone. Now passed on, AZ was killed by hitting a tree that had fallen across the road one night in a bad rain storm while trying to get to work. RIP, my friend.

Chapter 5
2017 TURKEY SEASON

Well my friends it was March 24th the day before the 25th and I could barely sit still and sleep for the morning of the 25th to chase the thunder chickens. There is nothing like a spring morning in the woods going after wild turkeys. But this season started out with light rain, high winds and storms scattered all about and cool enough to wear a long sleeve shirt. Tiffany and I were on separate place on my 20, I call it. She had a hen all over her and later like a ghost, one just showed up at my decoys. I never even saw it come in. We sat until 10ish but never heard or seen a gobbler. But the storm was kinda nice to sit through.

The evening hunt we went to a spot by my RV Park. We were rambling through the woods looking for sign and now and then stopping to work my calls, in hopes to get a big tom to gobble. On occasion, we would even set up and call for 20 minutes, in hopes one would come in. No birds, but it did end up being a good hike and we got some good insight seeing deer sign and also a fishing hole along the creek.

The next day out of bed at 5:20 a.m., I sucked down coffee and mopped up a big waffle. It was really foggy so I wasn't expecting it to be a great morning. In the past, mornings like these have not been that great. It wasn't long Tiffany had texted me from the hog farm, that there was one gobbling its head off but would not come to her calling. Which I might add was her first time trying on her own. She also had a lonely hen out front. After about two hours of this, I decided to move her way which was about a quarter mile away, all along trying to not get busted by birds. Soon, I heard him and rushed through a thicket to stay covered and sat up on the edge of a hill towards an oak bottom, where I guessed he would be in. Sure enough it turned out that he just didn't want to cross the creek. They do that sometimes. So after about 20 minutes, I brought him in for the kill at about 40 yards. He was a decent bird with one-inch spurs and a nine-inch beard. Happy ole country bumpkin and the first bird after 50 years of age for this ole man.

That evening we lit out late to Walnut Hill WMA, walking and calling every few hundred yards. Later we heard a faint gobble. Excited, it was time to move and move fast to where we thought it had come from. I bumped the call again and it gobbled right back and was close enough that we pretty much hit the ground right there. After 20 minutes of us talking back and forth, to our frustration, he just shut up and never came in. No idea why. So, getting late we decided we needed to head in.

About the time that I figured they must be about to fly on the roost, I decided to hit my Quaker Boy call, one more time. We were plum shocked and spooked when a bird gobbled at what sounded like 20 yards away. We hit the ground again and hit my call real lightly with a cackle and a cluck. Too fast the bird was on us at ten yards away through some high blackberry bushes. Tiffany shot but missed. I yanked the gun out of her hands and shot at it, pretty much out of instinct, two more times with no luck. Dang! What a day!

This morning was windy and pretty warm but I managed to walk two and a half miles without stopping, calling now and then hoping to get a gobble, to set up. Well that never happened but I enjoyed the hike taking in all the spring flowers in the woods and the sounds of all the critters while walking along the creek studying deer sign, pinch points and crossings. Also seeing some spots that looked like to be a chance at a few deer.

Day three, me and Tiff left out about 2 p.m., feeling positive but leery with it being hot and that it was. We had gone back to the 20 and checked the cameras and saw that there had been a nice gobbler there about an hour earlier. We set up about three times and ended up making about a one-and-a-half-mile circle, with no luck. Although we did spook a hen during the walk. While walking we noticed that it looked to be that we were gonna have a good crop of blackberries with all the green briar blooms. All the other usual spring flowers were out as well.

At about 4:40 p.m., we decided to run down the road to my 1860-acre lease, Wall hanger Hunting Club. We checked a few cams and there had been two toms there not an hour ago, on the food plot. So here we go with clucks and cackles with a few yelps and purring all together. The mosquitos on the first place was rough because we set up next to shallow standing water, so after 20 minutes we moved on into a place where the pines had been thinned, to try again. No luck. Of course, on the way walking out at dark, he gobbled. That's ok. I know where he is now.

It was 5 a.m., way too early to be up being that it won't be decent daylight until 7, but it was Tiffany's birthday and I wanted to visit with her before work. So, on my feet and off my ass, after a big waffle, I hopped on the Polaris and rode across Hwy 28, to the woods and climbed into my ground blind that I had set up a week ago. But first I made sure ole sneaky snake wasn't shacking up in there for the night. About the time when the owls stopped hooting and the doves were flying, I heard him gobble and gobble. He seemed to want to talk back but with an hour into it he just didn't want to come. After one and a half hours later, I was torn between staying put and being patient or going after him and that I did. When I got about 400 yards in, I sat down by a big pin oak and whipped up the sexiest talk that I could with my slate call. One gobble. It sounded still a good ways off, so here I go again. Setting up in a bunch of brush tops, I called for about 30 minutes. Now he's stopped gobbling. So, now I'm getting it in my thick head that I must have spooked him moving out of the blind and was seen. So moving out of the woods, I ended up coming out on a road where my blind and decoys were at about 400 yards down from me. I look down there and what do I see? He's there breeding my decoy, so he thinks. So I dart to the edge of the woods and move fast through them alongside the road until about the last 80 yards, where I think he is at. Moving slowly and drilling my eyes through every open hole until I could see and hear him. Barely seeing him at about 40 yards, through a briar patch, I took a chance and delivered him to Jesus with my Beretta No. 5, 3 1/2-inch 12 gauge shotgun. Wow! Happy as a pig in a watermelon patch. I did see how the patient choice could have been easier. Oh well, another good hunt and another good day. One of many and wish could have written about them all.

Chapter 6
TAGGED OUT IN LOUISIANA 2017

T agged out in Louisiana so I decided to head to Texas to Alan and Susan's in Dewitt County and Dustin's, in Lavaca County. As usual, I could have done without the drive through Houston. My stop at Jack in the Box for a burger made me wonder if I was in Mexico. No employees were speaking English back and forth and all nine customers that came in spoke Spanish to them. So, the lady I dealt with was as confused with my redneck slang as I was with her Spanish. Pulled my RV into Alan's place, visited awhile and then unpacked and slipped into bed unprepared. I was thrown off by it being just cool enough not to be able to sleep comfortably.

DAY ONE

We rode over to the hunt site and took a good look over the hunting area and fence lines. We saw one big coyote and three deer. Then we made a run to town to take them out to eat lunch and grab a few things that I had forgotten on my first stop at a store on the way down. Getting back, it had warmed up fast. Taking advantage of the time, I got flat on my back for a bit to try to lock ole eye lids down and rest up with the intention to head up for an adventure. At least that is what I hoped.

About two hours before dark, I rode over to the river farm and tried to cast a line with a few beetle spins in the pond, but no luck. While fishing I heard a few faint gobbles. So, I jumped in the truck and down the road I go. I opened up all the windows in my Dodge and sat there and listened. It wasn't long until I could hear them closer and spot them. There were six in total, four jakes and two long beards and man, did it end up being quite a show for the evening! The two bigger birds were at it and now and then both would stop now and then to run the jakes away from what appeared to be one lone hen. Poor girl! That night we got together at Alan's to eat and had some good conversation.

DAY TWO

About the time I walked out the door after a pop tart and a cup of coffee, I see Dustin coming out too. We left about 6:15 a.m. to what I call the river farm. We hadn't walked twenty feet yet when the woods lit up with the sound of gobbles. Close too. Being a tad bit late, we decided to set up closer than where I had hoped to. Now, it didn't take long to get the birds attention, but like the evening before, they did not want to duck through the thick fence, from the neighbor's property, and come on in. Eventually they moved on. So we moved down with them, sorta, and sat up in two other spots and a few times some gobblers sounded committed, but never came in. Now the action was amazing and so was the hunt but we just couldn't seal the deal. Eventually, the wind buzzed up to about 25 mph, so we headed in for breakfast and started caping out four deer skulls for mounts, later. Still didn't stop my nap though.

The evening hunt started out with winds pushing 18 to 25 mph but by 4 p.m., my ass was in the grass with squawk box going, prepared for a five hour wait. A wait it was until about the last thirty minutes, when a beautiful owl landed right in front of me to check out the commotion. Then ten minutes later, a jake popped out with determination but never gobbled. So, now I'm moving fast out of Dodge to my Dodge when I hear birds flying to roost in the neighbor's field. Then I see them in the trees. So it was good, because now I know where they are at.

When I plopped myself in the truck, it had gotten plenty dark enough to see lightning bugs and fireflies. It's been awhile since I have seen them, at least like this. Awesome! Back at Alan's home, we visited over a few leftovers then got on our backs for a night's rest.

DAY THREE

After making two circles this morning, trying to find the spot where I wanted to go, I finally found it. While walking in before daylight with my red light, I heard one lone gobble in a different spot, so that was a plus. So, I eased that way and sat up my decoys. I sat under a tree where all the limbs had just fallen off, kinda like sitting under an umbrella. As the sun rose, at about 100 yards on the tree line, I was shocked and happy to see what looked like turkeys on the roost. Sho enough it was. Soon the hens started cackling a little bit then gobbling started. So, I call back now and then and all of a sudden one flew straight to my decoys. Then another and another. Altogether there were five gobblers, one with a six- or seven-inch-long beard, and also four hens. Quickly, the fight was on amongst all the gobblers and when it was over, one stayed at my hen decoy. Man and that he did for over two hours. I took pictures and made videos. Gobbling now and then, I hoped he would bring another bird. I just sat there wishing and hoping for a bigger bird but it never happened. I ended up just spooking him away without just flat out alarming him.

Not much longer after that, I met up with Dustin to gang up on them, we hoped. So we drove around the other side of the cow farm stand, I call it, and eased through bluebonnets and other flowers, all along wobbling form where hogs had torn up the place currently and from years past. We just walked and called now and then. We heard a faint gobble and eased that way and ended up a little too close because we saw it. It didn't seem too spooked so we sat up and called and he would gobble every now and then but he seemed to be moving away. So, we made a half circle, sat by the edge of the woods and started talking "girl" turkey. Now it seemed he was getting closer. About that time, we heard grunting, hogs were coming. Two passed and soon a boar came out at twenty yards. Dustin told me to shoot and I did. He didn't drop but there was blood all over so we were sure that he probably bit the bullet. He ran off into a big thicket and we opted not to go in after him because he might bite back, since he is wounded.

Figuring that it ran our turkey off, I hit the call. Nope, he's close. Now I moved three times, trying to pick the right spot. Took him awhile to come, but as soon as I saw his tail feathers. I knew he wasn't a shooter. Nevertheless, a lot of action and a nice video for Facebook live. It was really exciting. I ended up almost stuck in the rain and bitten by a scorpion that had gotten in my turkey vest. But we made it out before the storm hit that ended up blowing by anyway.

Back to Alan's for a bit of lunch then Dustin and I rode out a bit earlier than usual that evening to an area we thought we had heard a bird. I was trying to help Dustin get his first by calling it in. That is really the only way to truly hunt them and it be a good hunt. On a full gut, we moved a bit slower and I moved even slower so Dustin could keep up. He is a good bit bigger than me and he was having trouble in some spots with the slick cowboy boots that he had on. Without wearing camo, he was a little bright with his blue jeans on. We had been walking and calling hoping to hear a gobble and soon did, with one that sounded like fifty yards out. We pretty much threw ourselves under the closest weistat bush that we could find and wasn't too comfortable when we done it. Dustin's gun was in hand and ready. I always carry extra face masks which came in handy today. Sitting flat on our butts, at first, we thought he might have seen us because there were no more gobbles and as close as it was, we had expected it to be on us real fast. Seemed like ten minutes passed and no birds. Then about the time I couldn't keep old bones in check, we heard not one but two gobbles, still what sounded like fifty yards away. Trying to make turkey talk as sweet as I could but we wished we had had time to put the decoys out. Plopping down so fast, we hadn't had time to strategize and move to a good location to set up. Unfortunately, we were unable to see more than 75 yards in any direction. Very lucky for us, two birds were barely seeable above the tall grass, kinda uphill. I could see easily though that both had full fans so a good sign. When I say baby steps, I mean baby steps that these birds were taking coming in. About the time Dustin was gonna have to rest his arm, I felt it was within range and told him to shoot. Boom! Bird went flopping and like many times before, other birds jumped on him so I grabbed the gun, with Dustin's permission. Boom again, another bird down to the left of his. Gathered up ourselves and eased up, both birds were laying when we approached. But just as Dustin reached down to grab his gobbler it jumped up and hauls off running. Now, this is when it got interesting because Dustin had to reach deep, pull his pants up and use all his old football skills he had to drive them cowboy boots to the ground and chase this bird down. There was no time to get the gun. He pretty much tackled the bird and grabbed it by the legs. For a minute I wasn't sure who was going to win this battle. That gobbler was pounding him and he was trying to pound it. The whole time I'm hollering, "kick it in the head!" Finally, boot meets bird's head a few times finishing it off. Dustin ended up with only several red marks. Nevertheless, we was stoked because we had just doubled up on two great birds with ten-inch beards. Both had inch and one eighth spurs as well. The main thing is that we had a ball doing it the right way.

This is just one of many times with blessings, of new friends and with the grace of God, to have the good health to make this good memory, out of a short life time, to remember. Thanking God every day.

Chapter 7
EARLY DEER HUNT

So one Thanksgiving week out of school, a lot of my family was over at my grandma's for supper. My Uncle Westley Williams was down and we all decided to go after this buck that my Uncle Jerry had seen.

Next weekend, about daylight, we lit out, five of us, to a clear cut in Calcasieu River and split up now and then. Since I hardly ever saw my Uncle Westley, I wanted to go with him. I think I was about twelve years old around then. This hunt I remember so well because I fell into the creek and was wet head to toe and it was a good thirty degrees or so, just my luck. We barely got started hunting so I didn't want to ruin it for us all so I thought I would just tough it out. It turned out to be a bad idea because I ended up frozen in front of the wood heater in pain from thawing out, being pampered by my grandma with cold water. I was very miserable to say the least and the ladies were not happy either. My feet were so cold I could not walk at all or move my fingers either. It liked to be a bad deal because I did not want to be a pansy. I learned a little something fast about the cold.

Chapter 8
TURTLE HUNT IN SWAMP

Three Rivers & Red River WMA
Richard K Yancey WMA

DAY 1

This little trip me and Tiffany lined up was to Richard K Yancey WMA, in the Louisiana swamps near Angola Prison and Vidalia, about thirty miles from Natchez, Mississippi. The WMA lies between Mississippi and Red River. Located in Concordia Parish it is about 70,872 acres or so, of very unique bayous, streams, lakes, mixed hardwood bottoms and a few cypress trees big as trucks. Thank God!

Many strands of trees along the edge of mystic woods like cottonwood, bitter and sweet pecan, cypress, overcup oak, nuttall oak, honey locust, blackberry, sycamore and ash. Now, our goal was to pursue an alligator snapping turtle in some back holes along bayous filled with vegetation. Of course, we knew being in the swamp in all its glory was gonna be a trip in itself. We left out late morning from home in Hicks Louisiana.

We had planned to go to a spot that my new friend, Paul Lemoine that worked for the WMA, told me about. It was about a two- and half-hour drive. We had never met yet. I gave him a call and like a lot of Louisiana folks, he welcomed me right in his home, instead of staying in a motel in Natchez, Mississippi. We ate well with them but not before taking both our boats out to the bayou at the end of Hog Pen Road. We motored down the bayou for Paul to show us a few places that we could set some lines out. We didn't set any out the first night but seen enough to be excited to get back out the next morning. Now, me and Paul have a lot in common. Quickly, I could see that he's a woodsman and pure American, in his beliefs and old values, like me.

Next morning, as were heading down the thru road on the WMA, we saw deer, some turtles passing and cranes in the ditch lines along the road. Of course, the beautiful sun glistening through the hardwoods revealing, again, that God has given us another day. We launched my little Pan Fisher Tracker boat, fired off my 20 hp motor and eased down the beautiful bayou. We were looking for good limbs or trees hanging over the water, to tie our lines on with about a No. 4 hook, tied with heavy twine like on a trot line for catfish, A small weight about 18 inches up was attached and it was loaded up with chicken hearts and gizzards and then we pitched it in to sit on the bottom. If you don't do that you'll probably catch a gator. Speaking of gators, it wasn't long before we seen some sunning on the banks, running for water and swimming. Stopping and fishing along the way, Tiffany was entertained a few times by some three-to-four-foot gators chasing her bobber within a few feet of the boat. We managed to catch a few bream and catfish. Then we moved on to explore depths of bayous and its beauty as we set lines. We were sung to in all the places we stopped by many birds. Later in the day though, it was easy to see that the day was not gonna stay bright. The sky was changing as well as the smell of the air and the way the water moved. Yep, got our butts wet fast too! Ha! So we loaded the boat and headed thirty miles to Natchez Mississippi for a motel room, food, gas and some good sleep. At least we hoped since we went to bed at 7 p.m.

DAY 2

Back on the water a little late but we couldn't wait to see if something was on the end of the lines. It would have been better to bait them close to dark and run them once every few hours after, but it's just too far away to do that. Now, what I forgot about saying, was that on the first day we bumped a log and my boat motor top came off and sank. Losing that cowling was the only bad thing about the trip, since come to find out, the dang thing costs 590 dollars. Crazy!

We think we had put out about fifteen lines or so. I have to admit it was a little harder than I thought finding them again, mainly because I saw so many spots I thought about using. About halfway through them, in a bend of a bayou, we got up a twenty-pound soft shell turtle and put him in the live well, Yea! Success! Even though it was not the one we were looking for it's still food on the table for sure. We ran into some more gators, some old turtle traps and an aluminum boat someone had probably lost in a flood.

By 11 a.m., it had done reached 90 degrees and got humid. We docked the boat on the bank and hiked in the woods dodging banana spiders. At one point, while looking for a hidden lake with no access that we could see on the map, we jumped a wild hog. We ended up finding it and it was a jewel of a site too. Huge cypress trees stood along the banks and their knees were over our heads in many places. Even in the daylight, the sound of frogs roared as we waded through the water, here and there, going slow enough, hopefully to see snakes. I always can't help but think about the moments of life from day to day that's being lived in these places, by all critters, out here in their quest to eat and survive. Only God could have created them to be able to live under these conditions. Later, we parked up at another spot for a hike and it turned out to be an interesting one. Because on the way back, I reckon that we somehow passed the boat up on the bank. Ha! So now, on the way back, we motored slowly through a tight spot and came into a beautiful little lake, about six acres. There it was deeper and we could tell that there had been a lot of gators there, probably because there was not allot of human activity there. Right off we caught a pretty nice bass and a few more. Then again came a good rain and made it even more beautiful. Luckily there was no lightning. While enjoying our slow trip back through the swamp, I'm thinking that Louisiana swamps or any swamps is some of the nicest places of beauty to see on Earth, out of 30 plus countries that I've been to. If God has blessed you with the time and health, to get off the couch, to get out in the world you should. Spend less time watching others live their lives and more time living yours.

Chapter 9
2018 ARCHERY ELK HUNT

DAY ONE

This hunt came out of the spur of a moment from just flat out being tired of the humid heat in Louisiana. So me and Tiffany had an idea to try and find someone to pack us in somewhere in Colorado. We didn't have a lot of luck with the prices. We had hoped to find something around 1500-1800 a person. However, as luck would have it, a friend I worked with in Russia, Tony Aloia, invited us to his camp near Monte Vista Colorado.

After the 896-mile trip, we made it to Tony's, bought a license for archery elk, went out to eat and grabbed showers before heading out to camp. They had a nice set up with their tents arranged so a few tarps could be placed over them creating shade, shelter and a place to congregate, in the middle of them all. We also met one of the other hunters when we got there, Troy.

It didn't take us long before heading to the hills with my bow thrown over my back and Tony leading the way to give us a start. Quickly, while moseying our way up the trail along a small creek, we noticed that awesome sight and smell of aspen leaves turning golden from green. Now and then we stopped for a chance to let our hearts catch up from steep rocky inclines, while climbing. As the evening passed the temps dropped with the cool air giving yea a little chill. It hadn't rained in a while so we tried to stick to game and cow trails. Sneaking up on something through the deadfall of logs, dry leaves and dead twigs is not impossible but tough. We came upon a nice little meadow and just as we got through it, we spooked a cow elk. We were happy to see some turkeys as well. Soon, up a rocky cliff at 78 yards, according to Tony, stood a nice bull elk. Tony had ranged him with his range finder. He was broad side too but I decided with the incline and yardage, I would have to pass on a shot, for fear of wounding him. I did make a long loop in the direction he went, in hopes of cutting him off, while Tony cow called behind me. No luck though. So we spent the rest of the evening stalking and moving slowly through the timber. After a little grub, we slipped into the sleeping bags. Tiff in her double bull blind and me in my Alaskan guide tent. The night was cool with temps right at 31 degrees.

DAY TWO

Up before daylight scarfing a few breakfast burritos down and with excitement building, we lit out. Driving in my little Toyota, we did spot a few mule deer in a meadow along the road side. We ended up covering a lot of ground through the forest scouting terrain and getting pictures along the way while enjoying all of nature that the good Lord offered. Tiff got her first sight of pine martins and also spotted an albino chipmunk. Pine squirrels were new to her too, they are pretty tiny little guys. We ended up finding some nice vantage points with excellent views but never seen any elk. After our hunt we went back to camp and met Roland. He is 72 but you would never know it. He is very kind and pretty much does all of the cooking. After some grub we take a little nap while the little pine squirrels raise heck.

Up and ready for the evening hunt we headed out to the first meadow that Tony had taken us to. Unfortunately, we only saw one cow and that was pretty much it. Somehow, I manage to lose my release this evening. I'm pretty aggravated and after looking for a good while, I decide to let it go for the day. So now, with only the light from the moon in the sky, we trudged our way out and back to camp. Roland and Troy had chili, fries and biscuits cooking. Always nice to have warm food to put in your gut after coming in from a chilly hunt.

DAY THREE

We're up and out before daylight again and unfortunately, I've got a sinus headache that just won't quit. Tiff hadn't been feeling good either, so we're both eating Tylenol like candy. On the way down the mountain, we get a little good luck and spot my release on the road. I noticed a spot that interested me while driving the mountain road, so we parked and headed up, climbing. We were happy to see some deer this day. Sadly, due to the dwindling populations you have to draw for whitetail and mule deer tags.

After a lot of steep climbing, we ended up atop a cliff with rocky unsteady ridges. Tiff got too close for a look down and I yelled, "Get down from there. You're gonna fall and everyone's going to think I pushed you off". She watches that Dateline and I've seen enough of them to know what people will think. We managed to get a timed photo together with nice view in the background. Someone had been here before and had made a blind or shelter out of some sticks. Remnants of an old fire was visible too. It was a breathtaking view. Straight down were tall pines that shot up to just below the cliff. The ground below was covered in what appeared to be large round rocks but looks can be deceiving from 10,500 feet high. It definitely looked like it would be a great place to see elk but retrieving and humping it out would be hell.

So back to camp pretty tired and looking forward to some shut eye, we quickly saw that wasn't going to happen. About the time that I got my Lacrosse boots off, one of the other hunters walked in, blood all over him. His name was Taylor and since he had just gotten to camp late last night, we had not met him yet. So up the mountain we went again. Four of us with packs on our backs for about a two-and-a-half-hour hike to a nice 6x6 bull elk, he had taken. Taylor said he had come up on a meadow and seen a small spike ease off and soon after a bull walked out. Ranging it at 70 yards, he started crawling toward it while lifting his bow over deadfall as he went. Then at 50 yards, on his knees, he drew his bow only to get pegged by the bull making it wheel around. While still drawn, another bull ran out in the middle of the meadow broadside, not knowing Taylor was there. So, he made a hit for a kill. He then tracked it for 200 yards and had to shoot it one more time. It was his first bull taken with a bow.

Taylor, Mr. Roland and I got busy skinning and shoving meat into bags trying to beat the heat, as the temperatures were steadily rising. Tony and Troy had head to town earlier so with only four of us, we were in a bit of a time crunch before spoilage kicked in. All the while flies and a type of yellow jacket, that resembles a bee, were hovering over the carcass. Of course, I had to get stung on one of my fingers. We all loaded up and headed out humping meat, horns and head. I could already tell Taylor wasn't gonna make it with his load. He insisted on carrying the head and horns plus meat and it wasn't long before he was struggling. I knew we all were going to have to pitch in, but then low and behold Tony and Troy showed up to give Taylor a much-needed lightening of his load. Tony immediately took the horns and head from him giving him relief. My girl did good and even though Troy offered many times to take her pack she always declined, as did the 72-year-old Mr. Roland. Very impressive and inspiring, indeed. Now back at camp, we scuffled for anything to drink and some gut appeasing.

That evening me and Tiff found our way into a meadow a few miles from camp. There we checked the wind with cotton balls and then I second guessed myself where to sit. The first instinct should have been the one we took because a few hours later a big cow came out to the edge of the meadow where we were gonna sit but here she is out of range. The sit was good though watching chipmunks and squirrels in a quiet picturesque spot that the good Lord had made. That night Mr. Roland made porcupine balls with deer meat. Also, three other hunters arrived, Chuck, Travis and his son Brayden.

DAY FOUR

Another morning and another mood. Sometimes on a hunt I get to a point where I'm kinda aggravated and set out kinda on a verge to hunt more determined than ever. So this time Tiff and I pulled on our Lacrosse boots, not the best kind for a long mountain hike but never let me down yet. We drove back down the mountain road about 12 miles to a spot Tony had said he had seen elk in years past, but he had not been to it in a few years. The first obstacle was crossing a river stream through thick brush and bog to the base of the mountain. Steep, steep. That is what I used to like because 80 percent of folks have no interest there and so it makes a quieter place for animals to stay clear from pressure. For me, years ago, the rougher the better but not so much now, especially with a tendon issue from falling out of a ladder stand, at home a year prior. It still bothers me to this day. After literally two hours or so of straight up, with ton of stops and about the time Tiff had about enough because her boots were bald on the bottom, we finally broke over some good ground. Right off the bat elk sign was there. Now midmorning, we were hot then cold because of the hike, Soon, we came into some small meadows, small streams and some quaky patches. Farther up they got even bigger and much more beautiful until some places turned into rolling hills. Now closer to noon, we were ready for a good rest, so we sat up to call and rest a bit. Most of the time it was as quiet as a mouse. Shortly after, out of nowhere the wind came up blowing all the golden aspen leaves off the trees, at 45-degree angles, back and forth along with the magnificent sound it makes. This is what I told Tiff is what I call Aspen Rain. I was glad to share it with her and the good Lord.

Moving along, tree patches drew tighter with mixed timber types and rock. Game trails grew more noticeable and I started to see trees torn up and elk poop, old and new. I saw enough that I fell into complete stalk and stealth mode. I had gotten quiet again. There were no signs of humans and it wasn't long before we did end up spooking something running through deadfall. It is hard to beat them. Soon we spotted a few mule deer, undetected. Then we came upon a wallow, mud and water, very well used and stunk of elk. This was gonna be a honey hole. We backed into deadfall and moved a few things out of the way with sticks, to make an opening for a shot, without leaving scent. It was 1 p.m. and had gotten a good bit warmer than when we left this morning. This was a place that I am 100 percent sure that yea could get an elk bull in three to five days, max. I would bet maybe even today, because it would be hard as hell to pack an elk out, off this mountain, and that is usually where I end up on hunts. Unfortunately, it didn't happen and we couldn't sit forever, we still had to come off this mountain. But still this was such a good spot that in the old days I would have hunkered down for at least one night, under a tree, just to stay.

Now older and with Tiffany with me and others at camp that would worry, we decided to come down. Now I never like to hunt back through ground I've just been through. I told Tiff this can be a challenge and even dangerous. Yelp sure enough, my GPS had from where we were and to the camp was 18.25 miles, straight line. GPS don't lie so that wasn't going to happen. Right off down the other side of the mountain, we were hitting everything we did not want to. Nothing seemed as it was. Low on water and not sitting much, I could tell Tiff was feeling it like many men that had run with me. But I was proud for her, and felt kinda bad at the same time.

One main reason that it was hell is because I was determined to figure out another path to this spot. The Garmin said that there was a bike trail about four miles away and GPS don't lie. I found that and marked it. I already had on my mind next year to take a motorcycle up to that point, hide the bike, then pack the rest of the way in. So down, down, the mountain ending up having to climb through rock a good hour. Now the GPS says it's about two miles to the road we came down this morning from camp. Just our luck, we hit a fence to a ranch, full of No Trespass signs. Trying to work our way around it, it didn't take long before we realized that is wasn't going to happen. I've always respected property lines but this time we were gonna have to go through it. All I had was a bow. There was no way we could go the way we came even if wanted to. Now as bad as luck would have it, about 400 yards or so from the road, we ended up right at a dang house that we could see vaguely through the trees. Thankfully we passed through without getting shot. Now on the road, the GPS said about four miles to camp up the hill and it did not make a straight line. About a mile away from camp, I thought I lost Tiffany, I was pushing. We took the last couple of sips of water and plodded into camp. I can say, in the good Lord's presence, that we walked close to 20 miles maybe more today.

Even though I was beaten, that evening Tony, Chuck, and I decided to take his Jeep up the mountain on a bike trail pretty much, that even a side-by-side would have hell with. This was one of Tony's little secret spots with some wallows. After a forty-minute hike down the mountain, off the top around the side, we got close. There was a fresh elk sign all around with trees torn up and the smell of them now and then. The first good meadow we came to, where Tony had just smoked a bear a few days ago, we saw a few cow elk. We sat them out and all took our places for the evening. After a short time, I felt where Tony set me was bad because the wind changed. So I moved and when I did I saw a trail of toilet paper going downhill on a stick every 25 feet also. Then another ribbon. Geeze. So much for a secret place. I told Tony and he was shocked. But with onX Hunt, nothing is secret anymore. It has helped hunting but I believe ruined hunting more. Chuck had seen two cows but no kills. Nonetheless, the ride to and from was an adventure for sure. We ended up getting stopped by a game warden with a game warden, Tony. He was just on patrol doing his job.

I died that night and knew I would be sore the next morning to even think about going to hunt. So, we rested and packed down because we needed to get back home anyway. However, we are going to leave with a spot to look forward to in the future and not be in Tony's area. Well it might not ever happen but it's there, you never know but it is as good as it gets and trust me because I have covered many many miles and days like this one, through mountains. Never be scared to push for a successful hunt. Sometimes you have to reach deep and bow up till you throw up.

Swampman

Chapter 10
ARGENTINA MIXED BAG HUNT

DAY ONE

As always my anticipation had been growing for a new adventure and also, my first trip to Argentina. When the day finally came to head to Argentina, I definitely needed the break, since I had about worn myself out with my new addiction, arrowhead hunting. On this trip, my girlfriend, Tiffany is getting to tag along, making this trip even greater.

We left Alexandria LA at about 5:40 p.m. for a one-hour flight to Atlanta. Then we caught a pretty rough nine-hour flight, with Delta, to Buenos Aires. The food was pretty good and the customs was not bad at all. Of course, not taking a gun along on this trip helped a lot as well as minimum luggage. Getting a taxi from the airport to the hotel we were booked in, proved the language barrier would be a bit of an issue. After some struggle we were able to find our itinerary to help the poor driver out. During the drive, we noticed the city seemed pretty clean of trash, however, the tragedy was many buildings, statues and even trees had been defiled by graffiti. So sad. After checking in at LOI Suites Recoleta Hotel, we took a 30-minute nap and then grabbed a city map. To avoid the language issue, we just pointed to places on the map where we wanted to go to the taxi drivers. Fares were very reasonable. We managed to chug down about a three-inch steak with a new taste at a local restaurant, Fervor. We then walked to Saas Nationales and then strolled through the Museum National de Culture. We saw some great art and sculptures. Next, we made our way to Palermo Lake, more like a pond to me but it did have a very nicely kept rose garden of many varieties. We checked out the monuments there, such as de Los Esponioies. I think they could do better by thinning the goose population though. It's a bit of a mess there with all that poop. Traffic is crazy! Also, interesting to see a guy on a motorcycle rip between cars at 50 mph with only inches in between him and the other vehicles. After finding Ntra Sra de Guadalupe church in the Plaza Gudemes, we say our prayers for a safe and good trip. We then decide on a hot tea and coffee with cake and a rest. Up and ready to go for a fast-shopping trip at the mall, in the Abasto shopping district. It was very busy and after 6 p.m., it seemed like double the amount of folks were in the streets. Black seems to be the color of clothing the majority of people seem to wear. Weather was great! It was just cool enough for a light coat now and then. Now, I started writing this story in the hotel because the noise in the hotel and town is very unusual for me, so sleep does not seem to be an option. Only catching a 20-minute cat nap every now and then but I am still happier than a mouse in a cheese factory, excited for the hunt.

DAY TWO

5:30 a.m., we are up to catch a taxi for a 20-minute ride to the airport for a one-hour flight out of town. I was ready. Upon our arrival at the smaller airport, I was worried right off. The speakers in the airport had stopped working, our flight was not yet on the monitor and there was a fire delaying all flights. The line through security was 400 yards long, for real! With a margin of luck we were able to make our flight to Santa Fe Argentina. It was a bit rough and rained the whole way.

When we landed in Santa Fe, we were quickly met by Davey the ranch manager. Our drive is two hours plus to Parana Sunrise ranch, but seeing new sights and getting to know each other made it go by pretty fast. There were a lot of old vehicles still on the road running, T-models, Jeeps, Toyotas, etc. Most of all the trucks were diesel. I noticed that most of what we drove by was farm land. Horses were still being used to graze down grass around smaller homes and farms tied with a lead rope.

We were met at Parana Sunrise by Miss Betty, the ranch chef, with a glass of wine. We unpacked and I unloaded the rest of the money that was due for my five days of hunting and fishing, to get it off my mind. Soon Betty whipped us up a beautiful steak lunch. Lunch made me fuller than a pregnant armadillo and it wasn't long before I was under the covers for a nap. Out of bed and in the main lodge. It's just cold enough to feel a little chill under your feet that makes you need a fire in the fireplace along with a light jacket. I sample some free spirits that I've never tried before and some calamari with lemon. We then sit down to a beautifully plated duck entrée with a decadent cream sauce and bread and butter. The main dish was steak again. No complaints from Tiffany as it is probably her favorite thing to eat. They do not ask you how you would like the steak cooked, it is always served medium rare. Roasted veggies accompany the meat and we finish the meal off with lemon meringue pie, very refreshing.

DAY THREE

Up and out at about 6 a.m. for a 7 a.m. breakfast. Then we head to the field to meet Leo, my bird boy. This morning's hunt will be dove and all the parrots I can shoot. Parrots are an invasive species here and destroy crops especially sunflowers. Many farmers hate them. Right off the bat the action began. Quickly, I was only about two birds for every five shots. For me, it's more about the action than the killing but I did get a bit better when I changed chokes and guns. At this point, I am using a 20-gauge Berretta. I am renting their guns for this hunt, which makes it easier to navigate through the airports. The parrots were harder than expected to hit. I can easily hear other hunters shooting in the background as well. I saw quite a few hawks of different species too. Tiffany about killed the batteries on taking photos of all the different kinds of birds while I was hunting. We hunted until about 11:30 then headed in for lunch.

After some good food and rest, we located some waders and lit out for a fifteen-minute drive to a flooded rice field. We waded out about 150 yards off the levee and stood in some cane that they had cut and arranged in a circle. Plenty of wildlife was to be seen. Argentina boasts about thirteen different species of ducks, such as the Speckled Tea, Yellow Billed Pintail, Rosy-billed Pochard, White-faced Whistling duck and many more. It's definitely an amazing sight to see them flying over and cupping in for a landing in the rice field. We also shared our spot with some big nutria rats. Leo and I threw out about ten decoys and pretty quickly, I was slinging bee bees from a number 5 load, out of the loaned 20-gauge Benelli shotgun. Of course, this evening hunt was hard to beat with the brilliant sunset in front of us and the full moon rising up behind us. I ended up with about twenty ducks out of fifty shots. Probably not the best, but I'm not here to win shooting contests. I'm here to have a good time from a good shoot. Unfortunately, the bad part was that we couldn't retrieve a lot of the ducks because we waited too late and didn't have a dog to help. But, Leo said the ducks should be fine in the cold water until the morning. Good deal since, many of the locals will take them to eat.

We get back to the ranch for supper with a roaring fire in the background. As always, we start with an appetizer and battered fried meat, um, maybe chicken. But who cares it's very tasty. Of course there is bread and wine which is always served with lunch and supper. Next, we are served perdize, quail, in a cream sauce, followed by fish and mashed potatoes. Tonight's dessert is dulce de leche and strawberry ice cream. We were beyond full.

DAY FOUR

We moseyed out of bed at 5 a.m. to eat and hit the road at 6 a.m. heading to a different rice field. Hopefully, to sling a little lead at some ducks. We've had a bit of rain since we arrived a few days ago so we met up with another guy who had four-wheel drive to get us through the muddy roads. It was a long rough road down, and we had to stop and walk in a good ways. After getting there, we set up some cane in a circle for a makeshift blind and then placed the decoys out. With the moon full, it didn't take the birds long to get to flying. Of course most of the bigger flocks were landing over in the next field. But it wasn't long that this beautiful awesome morning, so full of color and sounds, was messed up from the shots ringing from my 12-gauge Benelli shotgun. Also, I might add some splashes from ducks hitting the water as well. Leo was calling and Tiffany was feeding me shells. We were getting it done. I had to finish off a few on top of the water, wounded. Altogether, I ended up with fifteen ducks, even though, a few did manage to swim off on me. Great morning all in all! Tiffany did manage to fall in the water a few times though. Back at the lodge we managed to rest in the sun and play with a dog, enjoying the awesome weather.

Lunch was delicious and more than satisfying yet again. Bread, salad, deli meats and cheeses to start out, followed by chicken in a lightly flavored curry sauce. The main course was, you guessed it, steak again! We are in Argentina and they love their beef. This was utter happiness for Tiffany. For my taste, it was a bit too rare and after telling David, the manager, that it was like someone knocked the horns off of it, wiped its butt and laid it on my plate, he had Becky cook it medium well for me. A very tasty fruit salad of plums, apples, kiwi and oranges in fruit juice perfectly summed up the heavy meal. It's a bit chilly in here so we head over to the fireplace to warm up.

After a good warm up in the weather, we were up and out to make my first perdize hunt, with a dog. Perdize quails are a little bigger than our bobwhite quail. Leo's dog's name is Toby and it didn't take long to see he knew what he was doing. He took off immediately, nose first, until he caught scent of a bird. Toby would sneak up to the unsuspecting bird and then point alerting us to its location. The first time, I got caught off guard trying to get one off. Yep, the sapsuckers are out now- mosquitoes. Soon it was on, like Donkey Kong and I was blasting birds out of the air. This was more of my kind of hunting with sudden flight of a bird. I ended my limit in just under one hour. Davey said he was shocked because it usually takes most men about three hours to do it. All I know is that it was a lot of fun and my biggest worry was not hitting the dog!

I am liking the style and feel of this Bennelli shotgun I'm using. Having a small neck problem, can make for some aggravating pain from the shock of the shots these days. Headaches are among the worst. It gets pretty worrisome that one day I might not be able to shoot anymore. Scary to say the least. All man can do is live on and pray to the good Lord above, that He's got your back, and believe that He does.

Tonight's dinner was delicious again. We started with a sausage wrapped in pastry crust, like a pig in a blanket; it was okay. But the other entrees were perfect. Shishkabobs, ribs and lots of grilled vegetables. Bread and wine accompanied the meal as always. We are kind of getting used to the wine and not to mention the great food and service. Spoiled! As always the meal was completed with dessert. This evening we had dulche de leche mousse with meringue topping. It was a sweet way to end an already great successful day.

DAY FIVE

This morning, due to the full moon, we decided to take a fishing trip on the Parana River that borders our lodge. We headed out at about 9 a.m. after breakfast. Knowing that it would warm up throughout the day, we dressed light. Turned out to be a big mistake when we were shivering on the boat ride. Our guide was a young guy named Jose and he set up our lines and baited our hooks, at least at first. This river was famous for Golden Dorado and that was our target. Of course it is all catch and release. Using about a number 4 hook and wire leader with a slip sinker we casted out and waited. The bait we were using looked like a 5 and half inch leech, as we would call it back home. Jose says they call it morina. Quickly, Tiffany had a fish on the line and out of the water. Golden Dorado is a beautiful fish for sure. Then, soon another one for Tiff before I finally hooked a decent sized one.

On the way to changing spots, we ran across a carpincho. It looks kind of like a nutria rat but much bigger, they have those here also. Then, later we spotted about a seven-foot anaconda snake. Of course, I had to video me catching it and get a photo too. Not long after that we saw another snake about six feet long. We were told that this snake flares its neck like that of a cobra. Well back to fishing, Tiffany ended up to seven to my two. So, I guessed I got out fished! The river was beautiful though, and packed with wildlife so can't complain.

We are famished after a morning of fishing and a little exploring of the river. More than ready for lunch. Bread and a pierogi of some sort with a lightly dressed pasta filled us up good. However, we still managed to stuff some chocolate ice cream atop a liqueur infused cake in our bellies! Now we are stuffed and feeling a little rich for a week.

Evening fishing trip, well was pretty slow as I guessed with the moon high. Still we enjoyed the boat ride going through the channels, splits, and canals with all their mazes. All along the grass lines, what looked like, vibrant growing kelp mixed with many kinds of birds still shined in its own splendor of beauty. At some point, when it warmed up, spiders must have come out and spread their webs all over. Many were floating through the air painting a temporary look of flowing waves in the wind. As the darkness crept in they seemed to just diminish in to the night.

The rewarding part of the evening was riding along the river's bank searching for capybara. I think that is its spelling in English and in Spanish its carpincho. The first one we spotted, dipped under the water, just as we eased in, leaving with what sounded like kind of a grunting. Only about fifteen minutes later, we spotted a big one. We passed by it as if we didn't see him and then worked back up the bank with Jose motoring as quiet as he could. I was getting ready for the shot with a 20 gauge and buckshot. At about 35 yards, we spotted each other about the same time, so I let him have it. It was a clear hit, but he took off in the matted kelp, spinning and clawing to make a getaway. Jose gassed the boat up, into the tall grass, and jumped out, to try to grab a hold of it without it getting a hold of him. I stood ready for a second shot, if need be to finish him off. Unfortunately, I did have to but I was happier than a cat in a tuna factory for taking this strange creature. They are very large rodents, kind of like our nutria rats in the swamps or a beaver but bigger. We managed to catch a few nice Dorado fish before we ended our evening trip too. Now, back the lodge for supper.

Five new hunters are expected tonight so Becky has help with the serving. Appetizers like pizza squares and salad with a fishy taste started us off. Tiff didn't care for it, as she's not much of a fish eater. But she wasn't unhappy for long, when a thick juicy steak hit our plates. It was served with fries and was the best one yet so far. Completing the meal was crepes filled with dulce de leche and a burnt brown sugar crust. Of course, our wine glasses were never empty. Kind of funny that we are kind of wanting and expecting the wine now.

DAY SIX

I woke up sometime as I usually do around three a.m. and lay awake awhile. The view of the full moon out of the window of the bedroom, overlooking the lake helped occupy my mind. While we were fishing the day before, we saw a good many houses and small farms flooded leaving horses and cows looking for high ground. Flooding had hit this area hard and the struggles were painfully visible. It's always amazing how man, animal and plant will find a way to survive in challenging circumstances. It warmed up a bit throughout the night. The new hunters from Georgia and North Carolina came in a little late last night, so we did not meet them until breakfast this morning before duck hunting.

The duck hunt was great without any wind. I've learned one thing, not being an avid duck hunter, is that I'm in need of practice when shooting as they pass by. Now, when they're flying away or to me then they get in a bind quick. Leo said I was doing great though. I ended up with thirteen birds and one Iris. Feeling blessed to have taken even one Iris and more excited just to see one up close. Jose was happy to get a chance to try his knife that I gave him, by sticking and spearing an armadillo to eat for later. On the way back we ran into a spot where a hundred or more caracara were hanging out and seen a big bee hive and few more birds we haven't seen yet as well. It was a great time and I should have easily had at least five more birds plus I lost one wounded. Other hunters had done a lot of shooting as well but don't know their numbers on birds taken. We decided on a dove hunt this evening after a great seafood dinner. Great conversation as well with new friends that came to hunt.

Tell yea right off it was a very awesome dove hunt! I darn near didn't have to put the gun down. Super fun and super aggravating seeing I could use some more practice. I was using a 20 gauge, and it needed a full choke, I think. They seemed to be just a bit too high 90 percent of the time. It was crazy how about 95 percent of them came from the same direction and when I pulled the trigger or was about to, they almost seemed to wipe out of my line of sight. It was like they had about a 300-yard window of a flight pattern in the same direction and I was about 100 yards shy of being in the honey hole. Crazy! Nevertheless, I was amazed at the amount of birds that kept coming, sometimes up to fifty in a group. This made it impossible to determine which one to try and take a bead on, at least for me. I managed to do enough to keep Tiffany and Leo busy now and then gathering up birds and ended up with 31, give or take. I swear some of the smaller ones were pushing 70 mph! Ha! It helped having Leo keep the shells coming. He had his finger taped up to do it, with surgical tape. My gun did jam a few times but not complaining at all, with all the birds taken and an overall good time.

So, tonight the table was full with six of us eating supper. Pork rib seared and caramelized with salad to start, Main course was, not surprisingly, beef with potatoes breads and wine. We both decided on a coke tonight. Dessert would be the star of the meal. Flan served with a dollop of dulce de leche and cream. Belly couldn't be happier. There was plenty of after dinner conversation with everyone getting to know one another. We go off to bed full, happy and knowing that tomorrow is our last day hunting.

DAY SEVEN

We woke up very early, way before any light, to get set up for the last duck hunt. After a good little drive through farm land we finally set up next to a pond. We had made a circle again, for a blind, out of cane tops. The temp was about 40 degrees with no wind and we only stood in about five inches of water on a levee. This turned out to be a phenomenal hunt with me limiting out on 25 ducks while the sun was still rising. Using a 12 gauge with a modified choke seemed to make a difference and help me to redeem my sanity of what kind of shot I am. Ha! Taking four in one shot cupping to the water, and three in another shot made it quick to be over but I had a ball. The guys, Jose and Leo, were amazed on how quick and how many and how fast it all happened. Even as we were collecting ducks off the water they were still coming in. Sure made me feel great, 25 birds with just one box of shells. What a great way to end duck hunting in Argentina and on my first trip here. Another thing that made me happy while driving back to the ranch, was to see 90 percent of the homes and surroundings were free from trash. However, as you got closer to the city it changed fast in most places.

Our last lunch was served outside on a beautiful and warm afternoon. The lodge partner Ivan, opened a good bottle of wine poured generously, even more so than usual. We passed around the appetizer plate of a variety of meats and cheeses around the table. Everyone was very cheerful, laughing and telling stories. I'm sure the wine had a little to do with the happy mood. After empanadas and salad were scarfed down, the barrage of barbecued meats began. It was like in a movie. Pork ribs, sausage, beef ribs, and more beef and it just kept coming and coming and we just kept eating, drinking and talking. It was a definite overload on meat and wine and Tiffany would pay for it later. But hey, it was great food and conversation, with the other hunters. Of course there was dessert- ice cream.

Me and Tiffany decided on a dove hunt and she was going to give it a try with me. Like usual it didn't take long to start popping shots at bird after bird. The problem we had was most of them were way too high and we probably would have done better with a 12 gauge and full chokes. We could see some 500 yards away where they were pitching down in a field and I was wishing we could have gone there. I had no way to tell them because, Leo no speak the English and I no speak the Spanish. Ha! Real proud of Tiffany though, she done better than I expected and I'm very proud of her. We ended up with 52 birds between us in two and a half hours. That's way better than we do at home anywhere, probably. So good times! But, I'll definitely shoot skeet everywhere including straight for practice, before my next duck and dove hunt. Probably bring my own gun too. Couldn't have ended with nicer weather though. Unfortunately, there were alot of birds we could not find but vultures will make quick work of finding them along with other varmints. I wouldn't be lying if I said we've seen thousands of them. Crazy amount of birds are here like I've heard about all my life. Last night dinner was pork ribs and rice without my girl who wasn't feeling too well. I think it was a mixture of coffee, meat, cake and wine from the whole day, but she came out alright.

DAY EIGHT

Wake for a shower and repack to ride to airport about 9:30 a.m., for a two-hour ride. Looking back and saying good-bye to new friends and this memorable experience, was everything that I had dreamt of and I hoped my lady felt the same way. Saying goodbye to Davey was kind of sad because I felt like I had made one of the kind of friends yea know you can trust and hope to see again. We plan to try to meet up In January, after the Dallas Safari Club show in Dallas or Houston. Everyone at the Parana Sunrise Lodge was great and worked great together. Of course we gonna miss hunting the Rosy-billed Pochard, Whistling, Brazilian Duck and all the other magnificent waterfowl species that Argentina is so blessed with. Oh, not to mention we'll miss those fast-flying doves too.

Well, our flight back to Buenos Aires went fine but could have been bit better had I not had this kid kicking the back of my seat and screaming behind me. But hey, it was just a kid and a cute one at that. At the airport, we got a bit knocked back on Pesos because it was rush hour, about 75 dollars for a twenty-five minutes or so ride. We stayed at the Holiday Inn and after the high dollar taxi ride we decided to make use of the hotel's awesome massage parlor and spa. Spending time in the sauna and whirlpool, I like to always thank Almighty God for giving me the strength to get out and work for the almighty greenback (money), that it took to live yet another awesome adventure in, what to me is an exotic place. It was all great and then we ate supper there as well. I've never failed to see my blessing. Please my friends, see yours too. Trust Jesus Christ and know he helps those who help themselves faster, in most cases, more often than not. Of course nothing works without faith. We'll be headed to Santiago Chile for a few days and then head home. Live well my friends.

AKA Swampman

Chapter 11
BIG BUCK GOT AWAY
The High and Low of Deer Hunting

October 22nd 2017

With the first 40-degree morning of the year, I decided to go to a stand that I had not hunted yet. It's near a highway and the kind of place, in Louisiana, that you really don't expect to have our version of a shooter living. I had gotten two pics of him three weeks before and another about one mile away, about twice, on two separate occasions. So, I was kinda looking forward to the chance of hunting him. But first, we got to go back to about a week before this hunt about a mile away. He had showed up on my camera at that stand one old warm evening at about 5 p.m. for about fifteen minutes. So of course, the next evening I was there waiting on him. My eyes bulging out of my head scanning every detail and full of hope and anticipation as every minute crept by. Right at dark like always, like a ghost, a buck appeared. Quickly, I had to shoot and just as quick he disappeared into the thicket. I was hopeful it was a good shot with fair amount of confidence. I waited about twenty minutes. Dark now, I eased out of my box stand, on the fire lane, and slowly made my way to the spot hoping to see him or some good sign of a hit. Pretty fast, I saw some blood but not the amount I'd like to see. However, after a few rounds of searching, I found him. I was of course, thankful first off as we should be, to God, that once again an animal lost his life to help sustain my own. I feel blessed for the meat and for the challenge that all whitetail deer brings. Unfortunately, I was a little sad that although it was a decent eight point, it wasn't the big boy that I was after.

So now, sitting in what I call the playhouse stand, it wasn't long before five deer showed up. Two does, two yearlings and one nubby buck. Watching them feed through my scope, I noticed that none of them had dark hocks yet, indicating that they aren't coming in yet. So that dampened my expectations that a buck might be following behind. Although it was pretty comical seeing the nubby battle a bit with a cat squirrel. Keeping an eye out of my other shooting window now and then, I catch sight of a buck as I was glancing back to the does. His head was down and antlers covered so I was unable to judge his size. I did not want to shoot a lesser buck again, by mistaking one for him. Which turned out to be a slip up because I had a neck shot and didn't take it. He stood up and quickly walking away, straight away from me, I had but a split second to decide to pull the trigger. It was easy to see that it was him when his head went up. Guessing, that I would never see him, in the daylight, again I pulled the trigger. If only I could have gotten him to pause for just two seconds. I just felt terrible and sick to my stomach and not 100 percent sure of the hit. I can remember, a thousand could of's, should of's and would of's running through my head. After an hour or so looking, I called in my buddy Mikey Thacker and his red bone and set him on it. Still no luck.

Now, as I sit and write in the same stand, I'm thinking that my ballistic tip must have caught something on the flight down to hit the deer. I'm here again because last night, Nov. 4, with a cup coffee in my hand, he showed up 1000 yards away at another stand. So, with the good Lord willing me and my girl, Tiffany are hoping to get another God granted opportunity at him. So misses happen but don't let them stop you. Just always make sure that your gun is sighted in, you know the ballistics of yea ammo and try not to make stupid shots. The animals deserve it. Sometimes it's best to let them go and have another chance at them than lose the chance forever. Especially with bows and cross bows you should try to stay away from long shots if yea can. Good luck and stay ethical.

Chapter 12
LONG DAY FOR BASS

Thistory fishing trip on mighty Toledo Bend Lake, was a lot about spending some time with my brother David. Toledo Bend is one of the largest manmade lakes in America. Louisiana is on one side and Texas on the other. Over the years, its popularity has grown and with it many more people frequent it. In my older years, I feel it brings a heck of a lot more fishing pressure too. I think with all the electronics and more people, they just catch more fish and it is not at all better. Most say the Department of Wildlife and Fisheries killed too much grass years ago and there also needs to be more structures. Recreation on the lake has increased too with people just boating, skiing, swimming etc.

About four days earlier, I had dropped some sweet gum tree tops tied in a bundle with half a cinder block tied to the bottom and a small coke bottle to the top, to help hold the structure up right, and sunk it near a white crappie hole. I found that this was a natural whole and had caught a few there so I was trying to make it better. David and I stayed the night in my little RV that I kept at the Army Recreation Center, at that time. We woke up and chowed down on some peanut butter honey toast and coffee. My Bass Tracker boat was sitting on the bank lake side. We eased out of the cove and then gassed it for a mile or so and then got set up on the white perch hole. Right off the bat, we caught a few but knew it wouldn't be a lot because our shiners had died. It's always interesting to see how David fishes and catches them with one arm and then reels them in. His right arm was paralyzed from meningitis when he was a baby. The bite slowed way, way down but we sat a while trying, anyway. I even tried jigs. There was one big shiner in the live well so I put it on David's hook and told him to throw it out a little farther from the boat, to a bit deeper water. We both were just kinda sitting there off guard and had about given up when David's pole slams down on the side of the boat bent double over. He grabbed his pole and tried to reel it in but it was singing so I jumped down and tightened the drag and then he started to bring him in. The pole was whipping all about. Watching the looks on David's face was the best thing for me. I grabbed the net. Netting the fish, it ended up being a huge crappie with dark black markings and was beautiful. He was a happy camper! I ended up mounting it for him and it hangs in his little house in Hornbeck.

Now, the other part to this day was now that he was happy, I hoped to be too, before it was over, in something of my own favor. I wanted to bass fish so trolling and motoring from one cove to another point, creek channel and brush pile tops, I threw the world of lures at them until it was all my arm and hand could take. I tried wacky worms,

Texas rigs, Carolina rigs, drop shots, and spinner baits. Nothing, not even one hit for a good six hours. With only a few hours left, I had had enough. On top of everything, the wind had been getting worse. So I decided to go to the middle of the lake where no one was fishing much and see if maybe the pressure was less there and hopefully, have better luck.

Way across the lake we went. I got the motor killed and got David set up with a rattle trap. Then I moved to the back of the boat with my heavy spinner bait pole and tied a chrome spoon onto it. I didn't need to troll because the boat was on a steady move from the wind. We both hung up a few times now and then so I had to run up to the front of the boat using the trolling motor to retrieve bait. I think we lost one which hurts because they're not cheap anymore. Crazy prices, in fact. There was an island about two miles away and I told David that when we drifted close to it that we would go in. I've had more than enough at of this for today. It wasn't ten minutes in and a few times I felt like I had gotten a few bites through some stumps, so I cranked up the motor and went back up above that spot so we could drift through it again. Right on the edge of it, my pole dropped and my line tightened hard. I pulled and nothing really moved so I thought, dang I'm hung up. So I jerked back hard and about that time it felt different. I knew there was a fish on it. I knew early on that this was a good fish. My line was way out from just drifting. With my legs kicked up on top of the boat motor, I eased up and down now and then and let fall. I already guessed that maybe it was a bar fish or I snagged a gar or maybe a carp. Working the fish to about 50 yards, it came out of the water and I liked to crap my britches. I hollered at David, who was on the edge of his seat wanting to do something, and he did. I said, "it's a big ass bass. Give me that net." Reeling him in, the boat bumped a stump right about the time I was netting him and about put me in the water with the fish. Man was I stoked. The bass weighed in about ten pounds two ounces. I could have gotten a free mount with the Lunker program but decided to just take a picture of her and let her go.

Any kind of hunting, fishing or anything you want to succeed at, you just can never give up. Take the good with the bad and keep on keeping on. The only way not to win is not to play, so grab life by the horn and enjoy it when times right while you can.

Chapter 13
IDAHO ELK ARCHERY HUNT
ME & ROBBIE WARNER

Sept 9ᵗʰ 2017

Well this hunt came about from a trip me and my girlfriend made this past year on vacation, while passing through the beautiful Idaho countryside. I could already feel a deep desire to set my foot into it. The draw you feel to want to come back, to actually live with Mother Nature together.

So September 9 at 8 a.m., with my friend Robbie, who I talked into going, lit out for an 1847-mile trip. All went good for the most part, except a bad stretch on Hwy 287, around Dumas. What a mess, it liked to beat us to death. It looked like a bomb went off in the little ECO RV, tagging along behind us to use as a base camp, we hoped. Of course, the love bugs kept us busy cleaning off the windshield at each fuel stop. By the morning of the 11th, we was sitting at Idaho Falls at the DWF office waiting to open to get tags and licenses. Fuel was 512 bucks, for Robbie's part. I'll buy on the way back. I just put new tires on the "Olé plug along Dodge", but best she's giving us is about twelve miles to the gallon.

Now the main objective is to take an elk with a bow, deer is second. But if I get a chance, maybe downgrade the deer tag for a mountain lion, bear or wolf. Of course, the main thing is to have a safe good time and get anything. As I write, Robbie is getting a shower at the truck stop and me I climbed up in the RV, for what folks in the South call a whore bath. About to head over to fish and game office to get little information and license and tags. Mine were 950 bucks, with a wolf tag, just in case. Being a veteran, Robbie's tags ended up being only 179 dollars.

After a 96-mile trip to Mackay we went for a visit to the Forest Service and off to the mountains. The trip from Mackay was about an hour but had some rough roads for sure. We made it to our projected spot to start our hunt about 2 p.m. Tired from the drive, we were reluctant to make the evening hunt. I decided to get out though, man up, throw my spike camp stuff on my meat pack and head up. Up high enough to get a good vantage point, I started glassing the vast beautiful countryside hoping to spot some critters. Watching a hawk soar through the air in my Pentax binos was cool. I saw three antelope does feeding along the mountain and that was it. So, I set up my spike camp and nudged off to sleep. I heard a few coyotes or wolves and the wind during the night.

September 12th

Up and out at the butt crack of dawn with only my bow and binos, I headed up the mountain. I stalked within 60 yards of a big buck antelope. We didn't have tags for them though. You have to draw in this area for them though it was nice to stalk it. Of course, I didn't have my camera. The morning was just right temps though. Sitting among some rocky crops, I glassed under every spot I could. I thought I might have seen one deer way off and also a few mule deer were out. So I started back down the ridgeline sliding now and then, in scale rock, swapping form left to right so as not to tire out my body unevenly. Each time, I swap hands with my bow on my low side in case I fall, I won't bust it. Packed camp after a bit of grub and started about the two-mile hike back to the truck to regroup. Didn't take me long to see that I'm not thirty years old or younger anymore. My old 51-year-old legs twitching, shoulders hurting and neck stinging so I popped a couple of Motrin and took a nap.

Evening Hunt September 12th

We moved the RV up to an antelope pass, with a view any eyes would feel blessed to see from a camp site. After a bit of rest, Robbie went one way and me the other way up the mountain to spend the rest of the day. As I tad polled up the rocky face, I paused now and then to take time to smell the roses of sights and fresh air, plants, insects and birds. It wasn't long before I had reached a great vantage point along with a few trails and fresh droppings, so I huddled down, after changing spots to satisfy my ass. Soon way off in the distance, under a bit of snow left, I noticed some white spots that didn't look like snow because they moved. Sure enough it wasn't snow but two mountain goats. Later glassing the slopes with my binos, I spotted a lone elk nestled under a tree in the shade. About 350 yards off, he seemed to have antlers but with all the limbs, I never could be sure. A few hours went by, I even laid back and dozed off in Mother Nature's arms. Bear or wolves, even lions could have gotten me. I had no cares in the world, who knows what time it is, what's on TV (life stealer), or Facebook. I glanced over to see where the elk was at. Still there, so I decided to hit my cow call. It stood up and yep, it was a decent bull. For a bit, it acted as if he might want to come to me, but turned and walked away. With a gun, he would have been history. I didn't think I was gonna sling an arrow 400 yards. I saw some spikes later on. But the wind came up with slight rain and it got cold, so I decided to head back down the mountain. Later that night, I heard the winds blow in and at one point thought about leaving the camper. It was set up on the edge of the mountain. If it blew over we would be in a nine-line bind.

September 13th Morning Hunt

Out a bit late, but I don't have an alarm clock. We headed down a twisty, windy road just barely big enough for a four-wheeler. On the way down we spotted a bull moose about 35 inches wide. I shot him with the camera. Soon we arrived at the bottom where I and Robbie parted ways for a full day of hunting. Ever so slowly, I eased my way up being careful not to get my heart rate up too fast. That will give you headaches and fatigues you faster. I came across where a few trails met and decided to sit a bit and try cow calls. A little farther along, I was slipping through some quakeys. It was nice with the breeze blowing through the leaves and the ravens talking overhead. Slipping through some deadfall that looked like it had been created by a landslide, I saw some bear scat but it was a bit old. Already in to it, I'm feeling good that at 51, I'm still able to climb. Creeping through trails, careful not to slide on rocks or step on sticks through timber, I heard water. Getting down the water, I quickly saw a lot of trails from all directions going to it. So I rooted me out a spot and holed up in some dead fall and proceeded to sit. About 30 minutes later, it sounded like a mini tornado behind me, with the breaking of sticks and lots of noise. Yep, it figured, elk was bedded down not far behind me. I sit anyway, but sooner than I wanted I headed down the mountain to be sure to map out a trail, back to this spot, in my mind. On the way I was hoping to find one for Robbie too and I did find a big nasty wallow for him. So back up the windy road to camp, I couldn't wait to open up a bag of chicken teriyaki for supper and gulp a bit of water. Although, my life straw did come in very handy two times out of streams for water. I got a bottle that will hold about sixteen ounces of fluid. I drank water from that about four times throughout the day.

September 14th

Hard for me to believe but I opted out of the hunt this morning. Calf muscles are very sore and I don't' want to overdo it. But on the up side it was a good morning to miss because of the 30 mph winds and rain, so getting an extra wink will be fine. I wiped up a few cups of coffee and enjoyed the view out of the RV. So about 2:30 p.m. we decided to head down mountain for a thirty-minute drive. If you wait on the weather to be perfect yea probably never hunt. Busting through open areas, we still have to dip and dodge our way through mesquite trees even to get to timber. Truth is it would have been ten times harder if the cows, which summer through them, didn't keep it knocked down. Sooner than I expected I saw elk sign and even saw some deer sign. As sore as I was and the way my calf muscles burned it was hard to want to at all. Soon I settled in a spot that looked like a step in the mountain, with a good many adjoining trails, a good spot to set up a hunt. After finding a small log and building up behind it with some bark, small sticks and some rock, I got it where it was pretty flat. So, I sat my little pad down and applied my ass to it for a sit. It was nice for the first 45 minutes and then, slowly I could hear cool wind coming down the canyon followed by a light rain. So, yep, I'm out with my Sitka rain gear and my pack cover. Now my bow was between my legs and my release attached to my string. I adjusted my peep to make sure it was right and even drew my bow back to see the distance of my swing to shoot. Before doing all this, I cut and broke a few limbs by me that I thought might deflect my arrow. I use a Grim Reaper expandable. I like them in stalking situations because they won't unlock. After saying my prayer for a good hunt, I was focused on movement. I listened to the rain pounding my coat. Dark closing in, I kinda began to shake so I ended up leaving a tad bit before dark and headed out. Me and Robbie seen two doe mule deer on the way out, so we felt better about hunting here. Back at camp, I had Cheetos and a Capri Sun for supper, wrote a bit about the day's events and prepared to stare at the back of my eye lids, I hoped.

September 15th

Up to seven days with no shower. Wow, we getting as close to mountain men as yea can these days. Up at 5:30 morning with my cell phone on airplane mode to try to save batteries. The outside sounded like rice crispies in milk popping on the RV roof. Yep, snow and ice and about 30 degrees, with the wind howling, so I figured that I'm just not that mad at them right now. I sure was glad I decided to use RV as base camp. It is quick to see on some of these kind of hunts, who's really in control-God Almighty! So, Robbie came over from his tent and we talked about him and his experiences in Iraq and a few hunting stories over a little coffee and oatmeal. The hot meal was nice. All I can hope for is that this passes, but with it I hope it gets big bulls talking. But it didn't take long to see the weather was not gonna to pass. I decided that if by chance the weather set, we might have to leave the camper up here until spring. So, we decided to head down, shower, regroup and find a place more likely to stay out a bind. We weren't happy because I just had found elk. It took a lot of work finding some. Hoping to get to go back later.

September 16th

So, we stayed in a very nice RV park that belongs to the state at Mackay reservoir for the night, then headed back to the mountain. We ended up setting camp up around Muldoon Canyon. Soon, all set up, I started to hike up Glide Mountain. I followed a fast-running creek, about a mile or so up then split off at an angle where I climbed through deadfall until I started seeing some sign of game that was fresh. I almost had to wear a slicker suit from the snow melting off the trees and falling on me. Temps were about 40 with a light wind, so it was perfect for a climb. I only needed two layers of clothes and a vest. I was glad that I wore my 400-gram thinsulate boots, by Lacrosse, or my feet might have gotten wet. The bow sling was nice. I worked my way up pretty high to where the snow was melting. I found some cool rocks to use around a picture frame. I hope I take a nice bull to put in it. Coming down from a different route, looking down into the timber form above, I spotted my first mule deer doe at about a hundred yards. It never saw me. Thirty minutes later, another one and then another one except at forty yards. It could be meat in the frying pan but it's too early. About an hour later and about half way down, I cut a fresh elk track all alone. So maybe it's a bull. I followed it a long way and at one point heard limbs breaking ahead of me. I stopped now and then to call. Twice I could smell it but never had eyes on it. Dark coming soon, I put my arrow in the rest and headed down. I also, definitely saw a lone wolf track. It's supposed to be about thirty tonight so I'm about to suck down some spaghetti. Robbie watched a small hawk try to take out a chipmunk and then later a bigger hawk try to take the same little hawk out!

September 17th

It was so cool last night that I was blowing fog out my mouth from underneath my sleeping bag. Heading out late, we headed up the mountain and parked in a new place to scout and hunt down the road. Me and Robbie decided to go together. We ran across a few fresh tracks and worked our cow calls and I bugled a few times but no luck. Slowly, we worked our way up the north side of the mountain until it ended at about 10,000 feet or so. We saw some beautiful views and got some good pictures. I think I walked Robbie's boots off though because he had to tape the bottom of his Irish Setters to make it back off the mountain. We did roll some big rocks to try and flush out game below. During our scouting, we came across a huge tree bigger than normal and some rocks we had never seen before as well. A couple of good quick cat naps were taken leaned up against our backpacks. I'm guessing we hiked a good six or seven miles and didn't see any game at all. Pretty depressing. Dang.

September 18th Monday

Well at this point of the hunt, I'm kinda feeling down but still blessed to be roaming around in these mountains to see all of God's glory. I have taken a beautiful elk before, but it's been while. I chose to make a hunt up Howell Canyon, 10,768 feet. Dang walk just from the road to the base of the mountain was about a forty minutes or so. The first climb was through a big strand of old aspens. Their white bark is always beautiful to me. It wasn't long before I saw some elk sign, a little lower than I expected, and deer sign too. My thought as this point was, Lord it would be nice if the old man could make a kill here because packing the meat out wouldn't be so hard. Of course, this wouldn't be the case seems like I'm running out of luck, maybe. Over a few meadows and into dark timber there were many trees torn up by hooking from big bulls and bucks too, probably. A lot of droppings from both species and plenty of water, so I'm feeling a little better. Soon, I ran into some fresh tracks but it seems I'm unlucky always on this trip, to find them going in the opposite direction I'm going or the wind has been against me. Also, I realized that I needed to be out much earlier in the mornings, although the extra rest has been so nice and very well needed.

Nothing has been more challenging than spotting and stalking with my bow at 51 years old. I know the days are coming when I'll have to sit more and hunt anyway that I can, if God Almighty wills it. I hope He does because I believe He means us all to appreciate and enjoy the great outdoors with respect to Mother Nature. I came upon a small meadow within the timber with all sign I would need to sit up and bugle and cow talk and did until I got cold. Of course, it was already sprinkling and clouding up more and more with the wind getting stronger, to about 15 mph or so. Now getting damp, I knew I better suit up in Sitka gear and did. Three hours plus later, still going up the mountain near the base of a tree line and rocks, I called again. Now, the rain turned to sleet and snow. The wind was gusting up to 35 mph or so and snow was blowing sideways, which made it hard to keep off my face. My hands and gloves were wet from moving limbs out of my way from the stalk and holding my bow. Temp was steadily dropping. My intent was to be coming down from the mountain as late as possible but a different way than I've already been. I realized with these conditions that if something happened this high up, Lord forbid, I most likely wouldn't make it through the night. So, I decided to start down sooner. No one knew where I was. I had no satellite phone and the cell phone was useless up here. Being like it was, I had no sun to gauge the time and no watch. I'm hunting so I didn't want a watch. So, with all this, I figured I had to get lucky. But nope not the case, just a tough day of hunting to remember. When I did get back to the truck, my hands were so cold that I had a tough time taking my gloves off and even holding the keys to open the door.

Back at camp, about an hour before dark it wasn't long before I gulped down two servings of chili mac and cheese and went to bed. Later, Robbie and I both got back up and swapped all kinds of stories and then back to bed.

September 19ᵗʰ

Woke up to almost everything frozen. I reckon, I just don't want it as bad as I used to because I decided to wait until later to head out. We figured we kinda give up on elk and maybe try to find a spot more for deer at some lower elevations. This way it would be a little easier to track and maybe a tad warmer so we could enjoy the hunt. So about 1 p.m., we decide to bust camp down camp and head to another spot. It took a while, but we were blessed with just enough sunlight, along with us shaking Robbie's tent, to get it dry enough to roll up. We could already see, in the distance old nasty weather was about to strike again. So, we headed to the town of Hailey, Idaho with some info we gathered from a few cowboys that were unloading horses at a trail head to double check if all cows were down off the mountain and they were hunting along the way. Hailey is near Sun Valley and Ketchum. We headed down East Fork Rd. to the canyon. I swore not to tell anyone what the cowboys had told us, in hopes to draw blood on meat for the freezer which is safest meat to eat in the world too. Just before setting up Robbie to go after black bear, I saw a gulch that liked to have been cleared by a small avalanche. Meanwhile, I went up the road to set up the little Eco RV, to camp for the night, at least until we've scouted to see if we've landed in the right place. The terrain is a little more forgiving but not in an astronomical way. Gray's Peak tops out at a leg stretching, hip killing 10563 feet. "Crap!" We settled in for the evening with some hot chocolate. The "Swampman" now must be a mountain man and drop the pansy ass mode behind. Sleep or no sleep I was hitting the hill early. So the plan is by 5:30 a.m. to be up sucking coffee down to warm old gut for a climb.

September 20th Tuesday

Woke up to temps about 28 degrees at daylight with light wind and flurries already. I decided to head up a cut in the mountain straight up to the top to try to cut some time though I knew it would be rough. Wasn't all that long after I made it across a creek, to within inches of water coming over in my boots, that I was kinda thinking I might should have used game trails more because I was on my toes most of the time. The water crossings are another reason that I still like 400-gram Lacrosse rubber boots even on the mountains. Of course as usual, about the time I think there's the top, it's still further up. Like most cases about three quarters of the way up, I started to see some sign of deer and elk, so that helps yea in the hump. Finally to the top, I took my first snack and big gulp of water, sat back to take a few pics, enjoy the view and study the terrain. It was warming up quickly though making the flurries change into rain sprinkles now and then. Wind started to get all over the place. So, it's back to stalking really slowly and a few hours later down a slope, I saw an image. Yep, it was an animal and getting a few more yards closer, like a turtle, I could see it was a doe mule deer. Now, I'm considering the meat, although I decided it was a bit too deep for that to pack out. But I decided to finish the stalk just because and I got within 40 yards and drew back and realized that she sure was lucky today. So far perfect temps for hunting. But the wind just kept getting stronger and turned for the worst for me, blowing in the direction I was in which meant pretty much that I had to go. Now, tiring a bit quicker and wanting to rest more, I had to sit again and gulp down a bit of trail mix. About twenty minutes later, I heard a bugle. My first thought was that it was another hunter, but then I realized it was the real deal. So up and off my ass, I closed the gap a bit and found a spot by a big dead log, dropped my pack and bugled and cow talked. He bugled again and was pretty close but towards the wind in front of me. Then, I heard a bunch of limbs break so I'm pretty sure he winded me and he went quiet.

So now, I decided to follow elk tracks through the mountains and did for a good while over, down and back up two more splits, for about a mile and then I saw elk over the other hillside. I think it was about five in total. About the same time, I'm noticing a lot of sign all over and thought how good it would have been to drop camp here. I decided to end the chase and just mill around the area there, sit and then try to make it until closer to dark and did. Not sure on my route down or how long it would be, I started out a bit early. Soon, in wide open with a fast drop in the meadow I was on, I saw antlers to my surprise. I'm guessing forty yards away. I dropped down unhooked my sling snap, of my own design, clipped my release to my string and came up drawn. As fast I got the animal in my peep, I had to release. He had seen me and was wheeling and as fast as I shot he was gone over a steep step ridge. No way of being certain of a hit, all I could do is look for sign of a hit and quickly, I grew sick from lack of sign and was left uncertain of the whole situation. I combed the hillside best I could. All the time being grateful to even have seen one but sick at the same time. But that's why they call it hunting and not killing. With no sign of blood or hair, I'm pretty sure it was a miss. So, now for a long hike down and it's a good thing I started early because after finding a place to cross the creek, I got into a mess of a thicket that only a dear could navigate. I had to get on my hands and knees a few times to get out of it. I came out on a road about three miles from camp and thank God about half way there, a truck came by and gave me ride in.

Ended the evening drying out, warming up with supper and replaying today's events with what I learned and maybe should have done differently with the big bull. Most hunters go through this with a close call. But, that's what drives yea to come back to seek the awesome challenge and to challenge yourself on the mountain, with all its beauty. Ever since my first hike up my first mountain, it has called to me to come back. Like the swamps, the mountains is where I feel closest to my God for whom I love for each and every one of my adventures with Him and Mother Nature.

September 21st

1891 miles back, a long and tiring drive in an ole Dodge 4x4, bulking wind most of the way. Traveling is the first and last part of the adventure and just part of one. My time in Idaho was not lost because of no animals taken. I am just grateful to had been there.

Chapter 14

WHITE STURGEON in BRITISH COLUMBIA

June 10, 2018, was not just another day God gave me but a day to feel His blessings and to start a new journey that I hoped would be a great journey of another dream trip to pursue and catch a giant sturgeon in Lillooet, British Colombia. Driving three hours to Houston airport, we flew out with West Jet, for the first time. We landed in Calgary and then took a connection flight to Kamloops where we rented a car. On the first plane ride, there was a man with earphones on. He must have been tired because every two minutes for about thirty minutes he would sigh and moan really loud. He didn't seem to realize it at all. Even though many folks kept looking at him, he continued. It became down right annoying. Everyone was like, man fall asleep already. The second flight was a prop plane. These are a bit different. It was my girlfriend's, Tiffany Edwards, first time on one also.

Tired as we could possibly be, we picked the first motel we found on the Thompson River. We arrived at night but even in darkness of the night we could see the mountains. The town even had signs for bighorn sheep crossing. The fine part was that it was cold enough to wear a light jacket, which was a welcoming feeling from the Louisiana sun, Fo Sho.

DAY ONE

We was out and about, Tiffany and I tried to destroy the free breakfast at the motel before we lit out in our Budget Rent a Car, a cool black Hyundai. We traveled up to BC 1 and then through Prince George to BC 995. We passed through Savona, Cache Creek and Tobiano by Tunkwa Lake. It was cool and with the windows cracked you could smell sage well in the wind. Driving through Shuswap Indian land, I had to stop and meet some folks and did. We made friends with Oden, Mojo and Regina. I hoped to line up some swaps for a hunt or something in the future. This was all beautiful country for sure. Now arriving down in Lillooet, we got our first glimpse of the majestic Fraser River, where we hoped to land a giant sturgeon. Right off we found our cabin we had reserved on the lake and headed for groceries.

Still kind of drawn down and sore from scouting Lake Vernon at home, which had been drained due to repairs on the dam from flooding, I had to take my old man nap, I call it and got close with my bed fast. Waking up we lit out fast to meet with the owner of River Monster Adventures, Jeff. We borrowed a shovel and gold pan to try to pick up some gold, jade, cool rocks etc., and did. Later, we decided to take a drive out of town and glad we did because the scenery was very spectacular. It was rough country for sure. The view of Seton Lake was breathtaking, with a mixture of sun, snow and shade on the mountains across from it. It's the kind of picture folks hang on their wall. We continue down Hwy 99 to Pemberton and Squamish but did not make it to Vancouver before turning around. Back at the cabin, we were both beat and ready for bed but we had to eat so we fired up a couple of big cow steaks and a few spoonful of beans. I was stuffed like a rat in a cheese factory.

DAY TWO

Broke out of bed chomping some peanut butter toast and a glass of cow's milk. Then we made a run for the Reynolds Hotel, for coffee, to kill a few minutes until 9 a.m., when we meet up with Nick, our boat driver to hit the mighty Fraser River.

The first stop we ran the boat aground on a small island, dragging the anchor behind some rock. Then we rigged three poles with 200-pound braid, then a swivel down to a 150-pound mono tied to a half circle hook. The barbs were clamped down so it wouldn't hurt the fish if it broke off. Nick baited one up well, with about twenty cold worms wrapped with a string that looks like dental floss. Another rod was baited with squid and the last one with salmon eggs. A railroad spike was used as a weight made to slip with a tie wrap. The morning was cool, cool enough to wear a small coat and was windy, coming off the snowcapped mountains. It wasn't long before a pole got a good shake and I gave a jerk and he was on, my first sturgeon. It only took me about fifteen minutes or so before we had the camera out taking a pic and saving memories. He was about four feet long. An hour or so later Tiffany jumped on the bandwagon bringing one in about the same as mine. It took one leg of hers off the ground for a while. A good bit of time went by before Tiffany landed another about the same size as well. Soon after, we moved to another spot and got a few bites but were not able to seal the deal hooking one. So, we move again to a hole with a big drop off of a sand bank about eighty-nine foot. Not even a nibble for about twenty minutes. Then in a flash and with a dash of my ass grabbing the pole, the fight was on. I could quickly tell that this was a good sturgeon. Legs bent, back swayed and my pole bowed over, I was fighting to keep my feet planted on the ground. He was taking line and I was pulling line, then he would shake his head and run again. This went on for about twenty-six minutes. One time we thought he was going to come out of the water but didn't. Big game fishing at its best for sure. This fish was six foot and eleven inches long with a thirty-two-and-a-half-inch girth. Again, I reminded that dreams can be achieved through faith and hard work. Being in these beautiful surroundings with this majestic ole fish that I just brought out of the mighty Fraser River, is proof of God Almighty in all His glory. Amen. We moved again and caught a few small ones. They inserted a microchip behind the head of one, for future monitoring of its health and growth. All fish are released. No one is so hungry these days to have to kill one of these old giants.

Back at the bank, we tried to pan a little gold with no luck. So we decided to make a drive down Hwy 12, towards Lytton through Fountain Valley. Big country all over with magnificent mountains.

DAY THREE

This morning, after getting decent sleep, we were ready to hit the Fraser with Nick and Dylan, after a couple cups of swamp water and peanut butter toast. It was foggy and cloudy with a good bit of wind. We started out on a rock island in the middle of the river anchored on it. Right off we got bites but just seemed none would commit to it. So, a move was on and we slung four poles out at the edge of the current. Soon, I hooked one about four feet long. Then Tiffany got a good sturgeon, six foot and five inches. All the bites then slowed and about the same time the temps dropped a bit and here comes the rain. I told them it would rain because it always come with me. Now, they believe me.

We had a small mule deer buck pop out of the edge of the woods checking us out. At about the same time, I set the hook and right off I knew it was a nice fish. It ended up being six foot and six inches. Later, the rain cleared and we both caught two more about the same size and a few smaller ones. It was a good fight. These fish pull hard.

Hard enough to get yea feet off the ground. We was tired enough to stay put this evening, at the cabin, and grill.

DAY FOUR

Our last day was cool and foggy again, with looked like to be a lot of rain from the clouds hovering over the snowcapped mountains. We plan to head out tonight to be closer to the airport for a flight out at 6 a.m. So we packed everything in the rental car, which wasn't much since all we brought was our carry-on luggage bags. We gobbled down all the food and fruit left over, cleaning out the fridge and were stuffed like pigs in a watermelon patch.

Out on the river, for our last day, we started out at the rock island. We caught a four-footer or so, that had never been tagged, so we put a chip in it. Apparently, the only way to know the sex of a sturgeon, is to do surgery. We decided to do a bit of experimental fishing in some holes and areas that don't get hit a lot. Sure enough on one shallow flat, with a hole in it at a bend, to our surprise, one of the poles got hit hard and the hook was set. Tiff was up to the fight and that she did for about twenty minutes and then her arms began to give out. So, I took over and we had to chase after it with the boat, down the river, only to lose what we felt was what I had come for, an eight-footer. So, we went back and slung our circle hooks with the collage of tied worms to them and caught two, which looked to be twins. Each were about five feet long. Awesome! Now a few hours passed so we decided to go a ways down the river to a hole they said had been known for big fish, over the years. That was right up my alley. We threw two lines out and right off, one got hung. We decided to leave it there and see what happened. We were shocked because it worked. A good five-footer yanked it off or loose for another great fish for Tiffany.

Now, I'm still feeling hopeful with only about two hours left. We had seen a big red line along the bottom where my pole was at. I was snacking when my pole got slammed with a bite, so Tiff started out until I could get there. Carefully, we swapped hands so as to not get any slack in the line. It didn't take me long, after feeling other ones we had caught, that this had to be a big boy. After about twenty-five minutes of him playing tug of war with me, with me reeling him in only to have him then take my line back out with him, it was like he was just toying with me. I was starting to feel burning in my legs, arms and stomach muscles. Then he raised up for a nice little jump and we felt now was a good time for a little prayer because it was the best fish yet. A couple of times he managed to pull my feet loose from the boat deck and stay leaned back. Soon he hit the current and it got really rough so we unanchored and set the boat towards him down river, with me reeling fast, I could not allow any slack. At one point, the fish was ten feet under the boat and swimming upstream, at four foot, out alongside the boat, at 3 mph. There was no doubts about it since that is what the depth finder said. Forty-eight minutes later, with Popeye arms, swollen, we got him touching ground. It topped off being seven foot and eight inches long with forty-seven inches around the belly. Now I was happier than a bear on a honey bee hive, landing this very suitable trophy fish to remember.

Once again, I was seeing and feeling the good Lord Almighty's presence with this experience I just had, living my dreams through blessing. The mighty Fraser River, in Canada, that cuts through the mountains surrounding it, makes it easy to see Heaven and how real it is.

Chapter 15
DOG SQUIRREL HUNT 2018

Today's memory was of a cool 45-degree morning in the woods with man's best friend, after squirrels. My main reason for going that morning was to spend time with the son of an old friend from way back, Brandon that now had grown into a man. Robbie would also be joining us, a retired vet that just had two major back surgeries in the last five months. I myself, was limping with sciatic nerve problems. We all packed into my Can-am along with my dogs, Little Boy and Hop and Brandon's dog Yaeger and hit the road down to Calcasieu River swamp, by the house. It was kinda overcast and cool so it was a slow start and we wandered through the mix of hardwoods and pines along an old duck pond, waiting for our dogs to tree. They were wondering all around us back and forth with noises working overtime. They knew what we were wanting and they wanted it worse. Now and then we had to find our way through shallow spots of small streams and sloughs of standing water.

Then we hear them, "hah, hah, hah", and we yell back, "Get him Little Boy", just to reassure the dogs that we are on the way. Like a pack of wolves we scatter around the tree that the dogs were treeing in, with eyes glued to limbs up in the sky hoping to see a little bushy tail laying over the big pin oak, for the first treeing of the morning. Now and then dog and owner sorta talk to each other. We make eye contact and I tell him, "Watch that tree Little Boy" and he gives a head shake with a twice more excited bark, confirming the bond and trust yea have. Front paws on the tree, spinning in circles and running around the tree, I can't help but love seeing them work and enjoying what they do like any hunting dogs. After no luck spotting the squirrel, I decided to pull on the muscadine vine going up into the tree to try to scare the squirrel out. Yank, pull, shake yea go on the vine all along dodging rotten limbs and debris so the other guys might get a shot when the squirrel runs. Sure enough a gray cat squirrel lit out the tree to a pine tree like its butt was on fire and in an instant I hear a bang. Then a bang again and the sound of a squirrel coming crashing to the ground through the tree limbs and then the thump of it hitting the ground. At about that time, hunters and dogs all run to the area where the squirrel hit the ground. So the dogs get their reward for a playful hunt and we get the squirrel in the bag. Sometimes when there is more than one squirrel in a tree it makes it extra interesting.

So later the dogs were hammering up a viny sweetgum tree and we gathered around, gave a yank of a vine and from the tree next to it, a squirrel lit out. Brandon fired off a big 12 gauge and the squirrel trembled and hit the ground but was not dead. It and the dogs scrabbled through stuff on the forest floor but the squirrel knew right where to go, up a hollow in the base of a big beech tree.

The dogs were sticking heads nose etc. in the tree aching to get at the squirrel that just eluded them. The dogs were full of angry wines and desperate snorts. This one got away. So now with a lot of petting and talking to the dogs to get the dead squirrel in a tree out of their heads, we finally moved out.

It wasn't long they tried again, in a big cow oak tree. After catching up to the dogs, we looked for the squirrel. No squirrel but there was a big boar coon. After two shots from a 12 gauge, two with a 20 gauge and one from my .22 Magnum, the coon fumbled and slammed the ground from way up, sounded like a cow fell from the sky and yet was still very alive. The fight was on! It was the darnedest bunch of snarling and barking you ever saw. One second the coon had the upper hand than he wouldn't. Then came a time when the coon got Little Boy's ear good and sent him packing and squealing. Then like a rocket my young pup, smaller than the coon, hit it like a truck hitting a brick wall. Hop had him by the head and rolling around in the water jerking him one second and getting thrown another. This coon knew he had been caught. My pup was a natural born fighter.

The morning finished out with a lot more of the same action. There is nothing like the bond of dogs with their owners and good friends also. Squirell hunting has always been a great pass time with and without dogs in USA and still is and if done right some mighty tasty tree rats. Same for coon if know how barbecue it right.

Chapter 16
FIRST ARKANSAS TRIP 2019

T his little story started with a small post I had seen on an
ever so popular social media site, for the times, Facebook.
Scrolling through, I saw an ad for some land for sale in the
Ozark Mountains. Now, I've always had a little dream of a cabin in
the mountains. I was always thinking out west like Colorado. So, it
got me thinking, why not the Ozarks. So in the summer of 2019, we
decided to make the six-and-a-half-hour ride to go look at it. What
got my attention the most was that it joined the national forest. It

was located in Newton County and not far down hill was the Buffalo River which was a plus for other activities.

However, before we left, I did a bit of research on the area by calling the AGFD and the sheriff office etc. I learned that there is a bear season and growing elk population and decent deer too. The town close to it is Western Grove, with about a population of 320 people and sits between Marshall and Harrison off Hwy 65. So we made the road trip and tried out Tiffany's new Nissan Maxima also. There we met Brian and Jennifer Treadwell. They were great hosts and helped the owners, Barbara and George Day, show properties. They already have a cabin up here, hanging off the mountain with a million-dollar view.

So after doing some looking and some hiking of the property, we stayed the night and thought about it. By the next morning, I had made up my mind and decided that I couldn't lose. I'm going to do it. We ended up with ten acres that joined thousands of national remote forest land. Eager to get started, I began clearing a spot for a small cabin, making a view, scouting points and setting stands and feeders. So by September 27, 2019, I had a tent pitched and was ready to hunt.

First thing I did was to go down the mountain and check my camera that I had put out from a trip a few weeks back. Right off I was sick, but not real sick because I suspected it. Dang bears had knocked over my feeder and torn the lid off. It was a pretty bad set back. So I dealt with that best I could. Then I checked my camera and again I was disappointed. There was plenty of deer but no monster shooter bucks. Activity here had slowed way down. It was easy to see why though, there were tons of acorns.

Well the next morning I sat there anyways. Right off a young nubby buck came out and fed all around me and under me. Later a decent six point came out but I didn't drive up there just to shoot any old deer. So back at camp I tear up some groceries and change my clothes into ones that I had sprayed with permethrin spray, the day before, to keep the ticks off. Then I headed down the mountain with a can of red spray paint and some glow in the dark stickers to discretely mark me some trails, in the National Forest, for future hunts. On and in my place are a lot of beautiful rocky outcrops. As I pass by and under them, I'm being careful not to spook two things, bears with cubs that

I got on my camera, and rattlesnakes. Using Google Earth and GPS to help me measure distances and look for routes to the river and pinch points that lead game to one point. Now and then I find a spot where I just have to stop and take in how thankful I am, and I am reminded how with faith and hard work and God's will, that I just might happen to have a little cabin here.

Back at camp, I worked on getting a water line down the mountain to the cabin site. Now, I'm dying for water so that I could clean up. We were lucky to get water but the power is way too far off and I am fine with that. So, I cleaned up best that I could with a rag and water and baby wipes and changed clothes.

Heading to the stand, for the first evenings hunt, I jumped a deer. I wasn't in my lock in stand long when the squirrels almost took me out. Acorns were flying out of the shaken limbs, they were jumping on, and then gathering them up for the winter. This was good, I hadn't seen squirrels like this back home in years. Then I heard steps behind me. I about broke my neck and caused my eyeballs to lock, wanting to look straight behind me to see what it was. Usually, it is best to sit still and let whatever it is walk past. But I could tell they were going in the wrong direction so they had to turn. It ended up being three big ole nanny does. Other than a praying mantis crawling on my stand and some owls hooting that was it for the day.

I got in my ladder stand, for the second morning hunt, just about the time that I didn't need a light. Well, I wasn't alone this morning, I had a squirrel in the tree with me right above my head. Apparently, he wasn't very happy to see something in his way to start his morning off so he barked at me for ten minutes before I had to show him that I was bigger than him. It was actually cool enough that I wished I had worn a long sleeve shirt for sure. Later, I was visited by a small spike that wrestled with eating the acorns off a white oak near my Sweeney feeder. I finished out the morning at about nine then hiked up the hill to eat a small second breakfast.

Changing clothes first, I lit out to so do some hiking to see more. I loved the area with its diverse and changing terrain. An hour or so later I had made my way down to the edge of the Buffalo River, on a high bluff looking down at the clear blue waters, with visibility for half a mile in both directions. After resting my legs a bit, I followed alongside the river best I could until I seen what looked like a slope heading down. After a bit, I found a way down to the river bank and explored the rocky edges. All along I spotted some nice fresh elk tracks, beautiful rocks, cool drift wood where the river had torn trees off the banks and more. I decided to try a little different route up the mountain. Yelp, it was thicker, steeper and rockier. Along the way, I picked up a good mess of seed ticks that I happened to see on my gray Magellan fishing pants. I grabbed a limb and beat them off my legs. By the time I got back to camp I was worn, tired and hungry again. But first, I stripped down and got under the water hose. Man what a blessing running water is. Now clean and full, a good nap was in order under the shade of a giant oak tree at my camp.

The evening hunt was warm and windy. I did not see any deer but had two gray foxes come out and eat some bait I had out for the bears. It was good to have gotten to see them. The evening ended with a good long squirrel fight.

My third morning hunt started with one small yearling coming out. At first the wind was beating through the tree limbs and leaves a bit then just like that it got calm, still and quiet. Not long into it and like a ghost, a black bear appeared and walked twenty yards by me up to the bait. It got a good sniff and decided that something was not quite right and slipped off real slow and quiet and stealthy as it could. It was too small I thought, to shoot and I had not checked the quota in a few days anyhow. I finished out the morning and made a little hike into an area that I had not been and came upon a post oak ridge. There were some fresh rubs and scrapes to my surprise being so early but I figured it must be some young buck's first year and he didn't know that it was probably too early to get him a girlfriend.

Afternoon and I was back for my old man nap and some grub in my tummy. After I awoke I decided to get under that water hose. So standing there naked in the wide open, seventy or so yards out, two deer are standing there looking at me. They stared at me for a while and I thought it was pretty hilarious and figured they never quite seen a set of nuts like these.

So grabbed up my little beach chair equipped with slings to put on my back and pocketed what things I needed out of my backpack then made my way through the rocks to the little oak ridge with scrapes. After about thirty minutes of trying to decide where the best place could be, I set down by a big dead tree for cover. Now, even then I thought that this would be a great place for a snake. A few minutes after it got quiet and I thought close to a dozen squirrels were gonna get in my lap. I was still and attentive to every sound and movement, being on the ground you have to. Out of the corner of my eye, three deer passed. Then dark fell. As I gathered up my stuff, sure enough a rattlesnake slithering about a foot from where I was just sitting. Yea would think that I would trust my instincts more.

My final day, I spent clearing some deadfall away from the cabin spot. I made the morning and evening hunt but only seen a few does. So it was a good start for a good dream to have my own little spot in the world, in the mountains somewhere. So Western Grove Arkansas, it's gonna be, it looks like, for a start.

Now by 2023 I have 13 acres here with a main and guest cabin complete and have had quite a few adventures there on Buffalo River and more with taking a nice six-and-a-half-year-old black bear. At 57 years young now, I hope to pass 70 with the good Lord's grace. I can always use prayers.

Chapter 17
AFRICA 2019

08/15/2019

S
o this adventure started like some had before, when me and Tiffany went to the Dallas Safari Convention in January 2019. I had not really planned to book anything, just enjoy the show. As always, it was full of adventures to be found. It wasn't long I found myself buying a new pair of binos with a built-in range finder. Something I would have loved to have had in days gone by. After passing on a wolf hunt and another exploratory trip to the Amazon, I ran across Reiner and Lad Shunneson Adventurers, and seen that they would be willing to set up a small game safari. This was a lot of animals that I wanted to take in the past but other outfitters were not really interested.

So now it's August and we are getting on a plane in Houston, Texas for our first fourteen-hour flight, east to Doha. The closer we get, the more excited I got but also redder eyed and tired. Sleeping on a plane is rough on me. The first meal was okay, with slow cooked beef in caramelized onion sauce with all the trimmings. Flying with Qatar Air and they seemed to be doing a good job although, upon loading I felt a bit uncomfortable from folks that I saw boarding. Once in Doha airport, right off I was impressed. One of the best I have ever seen, It wasn't long we went through security and got a taxi and set out to see what we could of the city. We had a nine plus hour layover so we decided that just looking at the airport wasn't an option. Right off we noticed a lot of roads being built, buildings etc. We found out that they were bidding to host the 2020 Olympics. They were also close to completion of an underground metro. They had built a very impressive coliseum with real unusual architecture. We started out at the market, Souq Waqif. This is where the rich folks shop. There is some big money in this town. Of course we had to take the little boat ride like the ones they have in Venice Italy, the difference being this was inside the building. We tore up some good crepes while there and scoped out this sweet spot for a bit. Easy to see and feel we were surely not at home with folks in there Islamic clothes, hijabs etc., with their faces and heads covered. The population is diverse and includes Indians, Pakistanis, Arabs and many more. Because of this, the attire is just as diverse as the population. One thing we noticed that there was very little smoking, no drunks, in fact not even a liquor store. The next market we went to was, I think, one of the biggest ones I've seen in all my places that I have been. It was more geared for everyone with everything. A lot of cafes, restaurants, kiosks and of course tourist's items. We even ran into a taxidermy shop. Work was lacking to say the least though. Now dark, the lights of the city shined bright. I was very impressed with the tall street poles with lights that lit up from the top to the bottom and changed colors now and then.

Boarding now and on the way to Johannesburg. We landed about daylight. The flight was about nine hours long. A few movies, a meal and a lot of head bobbing later, we were glad to finally be there. After grabbing our luggage we met Dion, our guide and headed out for a four-hour drive to our fist lodge. I've always loved the little Toyota diesel trucks and they seem to be popular here. The drive down there was pretty much no way I was going to be able to keep my head up and try not to fall asleep, I wasn't much even wanting to talk either. We also met up with our cook, Pricilla and then tracker, Timba, who met us there. Arriving at the lodge, it didn't take me long until I make my self-known to the bed. It was all I wanted at the moment. As fast as I hit the bed it seemed like there was a knock on the door for supper. Grilled chicken with a lot of fixings to go with it and topped out with a glass of wine.

DAY ONE

The night's rest was okay, but not great. Out of bed at six a.m., for breakfast. Morning was cool enough to wear a light coat and windy. Sunrise was great through the hills and could see a good bit of game already. We went out to the gun range to test fire the .300 and .243. For most of what I'm after the .243 will be plenty sufficient. It will just leave a small hole so each animal can be mounted. We're staying in Vrede which means peace, at Driekoppen, a farm in the Eastern Free State of South Africa. There are a lot of farms here and that is why we are here because a lot of the game I'm after lives around farmland. While riding around a bit we saw a lot of plains game. The wind whipping the golden grass had it looking like the waves on a lake.

Soon I made my first kill of an Egyptian Goose. I had my eye on a mongoose but the wind kept most of them at bay in the holes. Later in another hole we got into some ducks, it was fun to watch JD, Dion's Jack Russell terrier swim out to try to retrieve them.

Back at the lodge, we had a nice brunch and that set the mood for a good nap that I hoped would prepare me for my first night hunt. So the first night was cool and windy with a full moon. We loaded up in the Helix turbo diesel six speed and headed out. Me and Timba in the back of the truck, locked and loaded. Timba had a spot light scouring the mountain side. We saw a lot of game. We came across a few skunks but they were a bit too fast to get back in their holes before we could get close enough for a shot. I saw a lot of mountain reed buck, duikers and steenboks through the scope but I was hoping for a caracal or serval. Soon and with a lot of luck I had one in my scope, about 150 yards, but all I could see was a head and ears. I couldn't really tell where the body was. Soon he had all he could take with a light in his eyes and took off across a small canyon, now he was close to 225 to 250 yards and moving. I turned the scope down and squeezed off a shot and it was a hit from the sound of it. So we unloaded JD, the Jack Russell, and lit out. It was good to see blood pretty close right off the bat. About twenty minutes into it, I saw him in a tree and not taking any chances to lose it, I blasted it with the shotgun sending it flopping through the trees to the ground. JD was all over it. I was pumped with this being my primary target for this trip, a serval. Very excited, big cat also.

Later, I took a spring hare with the .243, at about 300 plus yards, very unusual and cool looking critter. An hour or so later I added a cape fox to my take and also ending the first night's hunt. Three shots and three kills. Later, we got to see an aardvark up close and personal.

DAY TWO

A few hours of sleep and we were up and out to meet with some other trackers and a dog handler to bust out into some canyons. That we did with thirteen dogs, blue ticks, plots, walkers, black and tans and greyhounds, which were the catch dogs. We stayed high on the canyon, moving every now and then just ahead of the dogs. Soon, we saw a black backed jackal but he cut a rug in the wrong direction with dust trail following his ass, so we never got up to him but tried. Out of luck for the day hunt, we hoped for better luck tonight.

So, that night we drove about an hour and a half down to a different province, with the primary target being a black backed jackal, using a light not the dogs though. Some species can only be hunted in other areas. There, we meet with the rancher to ride along on his 4000 plus acre ranch. Right away we saw a beautiful sight but it was not good. A huge wild fire was eating up the dry grasses off in the distance. The strong winds were trying to pop my hat off my head, now and then, as I sat in the seat in the back of the truck where Timba was working the light for me. I had the .243 locked and loaded. In the first hours, we seen very little game but as the wind died down, more and more began to move, Steenbok, duiker and rabbits were out and about. Soon we spotted an Aardwolf at about 250 yards. I decided to try and take him but really all I could see was his head and eyes. I guessed which way his body was but guessed wrong, a miss. I slung one more down range again while he was in a run, but no luck. Thankfully, about forty minutes or so later, we came across another one. It moved now and then but finally stopped. So, I cranked the scope up and with it resting on a pack across the cab of the truck, I squeezed off a shot and it sounded like a hit. But then it lit out like a bat out of hell zigzagging through the tall grasses. We rode around to look but with no luck. So, the next move was to set JD out at the spot where I last shot it. He was on the trail and gone with us running behind him and soon we hear a fight coming on. The aardwolf was wounded and it was something to see. The mane of hair going down his back was standing up to make it appear much bigger. As quick as I could and safe as I could, I finished it off with Dion's pistol. It was different seeing it in real life than in a picture. On the way coming off the ranch we saw two more. By the time we got back to the lodge, I could not wait to hit the bed for about five hours sleep before it would be time to go again.

DAY THREE (Black Backed Jackal)

This morning we ate and was just out past the butt crack of daylight, feeling kinda happy that dang wind had slowed some. We met the houndsman, Moses, and his pack dogs and hit the long canyon with a nice bit of vegetation and rocky slopes. It wasn't too long when we heard the dogs jump and then we saw two bush pig boars running across the hill at 580 yards, according to my new Lica binos. I wasn't really interested in the pigs, because I had already taken some in past trips. So after moving a few times, to keep up with Moses and his dogs, we both were in a spot to see the dogs strike and run into a wooded rocky out crop and then they just kinda stopped. Soon, Moses radioed us that they had one treed. So, off we go Dion, Tiffany and me. When we got to them, the dogs were in a cave, so deep that we had to be no more than ten feet from the entrance to hear them. Now, the entrance was about a four-foot diameter and tapered down to size that the dogs had to lay sideways and drag themselves, scratching their way in. Four or five came out and it was shocking to see them do it. Kinda happy and sad, I was curious to see how the heck we were ever gonna get this thing out, if ever. Now, calling and keeping all the dogs out was a long process. Hour or so later, we had gotten it down to two dogs in, they just weren't going to quit, Prince, a walker and Jack, a jack russell. You can hear the jackal growling and snarling back at the dogs and an occasional fight. They are a bit like a coyote but a bit smaller and colored differently. They push prey in these holes and dig it out to kill it. This time the tide was turned for sure. After a good thirty minutes or more Dion decided to go in as deep as he could, belly crawling and got in enough so all that could be seen was his feet. Still no luck, so Moses went in after Dion to try and still no luck. So he got a piece of barb wire and Dion went back in, twisting it trying to probe the dogs out or tangle the jackal's tail with it. This seemed at first like it was working but the jackal would just not come out. Now, they decided to bring in what they called "the last resort" a one-eyed jack russell, named Moolly. He is very effective but just won't quit. It wasn't long it sounded like all hell broke loose and at one point everyone drew back as Dion was yelling to pull him out. We thought he was about to unass that cave. But he still went back in turning barb wire and ended up dragging the jackal out with the fight for me to shoot it with his pistol. Poor bully dog was torn up on his head, ears, and face but not severe. All the dogs pretty much showed scars of past encounters but it's what they love and live to do. So after all of this, I plan to full body mount this jackal to honor its memory of the adventure and its beauty. Again, we hunt some animals, like this one, to keep them in check and to save hundreds of small lambs through the year.

So tonight was a bit cooler with a light wind, altogether with the truck moving, it made it just enough to not be comfortable, but we hung in there for a while. Then the fog rolled in and the moon was full, so the spotlight wasn't that effective. We came across why we are hunting these predators, it was a young springbok that had been killed and partially eaten. Also, seen where an ostrich had laid an egg the size of my head or darn near it. There wasn't much moving, so we decided to call it a night.

DAY FOUR (Ducks and Mongoose)

We slept in a bit then revisited some bacon and eggs. Me and Tiff were nestled back against some big rocks at the edge of one of the small lakes, after a failed attempt to shoot a huge goose, two yellow billed ducks flew in and I touched off two rounds, taking one of them. Then we rode around trying to get a ground squirrel. This was fun and challenging with me trying to shoot the twelve-gauge Benelli out the back of the truck, pushing ten miles per hour. I did hit one but it dipped in its hole so I lost it, but did end up getting a nice mongoose. We didn't stay long because I had a hunt tonight also.

Tonight we made about an hour drive to hunt porcupines and skunk on some huge cut corn fields, near Reiner's old home place as a kid. Tonight was perfect for weather, just being cool enough from time to time, to get a chill, with no wind. Soon we spotted some wild guinea fowl and chased them through the field with the shotgun shooting at them in flight and the truck moving. Missed the first bird but later redeemed myself. It had a huge horn for an old bird. Themba was happy to take it home for supper later.

Then I got into my first African porcupines, taking them the same way, hauling butt shooting from the back of the truck. We ended up with six, I think. Tiffany took her first also. It was so much fun watching her learn to hit them. Porcupines are extreme nuisances here and destroy farmland which is precious for obvious reasons, so you can kill as many as possible. If you shoot five, five will be back the next day. I do plan to mount all the animals I take, myself.

We've been hunting elevations between 5000 and 6500 feet. We saw a lot of steenbok, blesbok and a serval cat that was hunkered down in the grass trying to slip away without being seen. Later two more, one on the river's edge giving us time to look him over good in the binos under the spot light. Reiner said he saw his first one when he was eighteen years old but now he sees them every night. The caracal is a little harder to see.

Soon, we spotted a black and white fur ball bouncing through the old corn field. We rushed it with truck and at about 55 yards and I ended up taking a skunk, pole cat, with one shot. Stinky but beautiful critter, we carefully got a few pics, then bagged it to take to the taxidermist, where they will skin it, dip it, pack and send to me in the States. We were out until two in the morning, so I had no problem getting flat on my back for some sleep in la la land.

DAY FIVE

Packed, ate and headed out to Limpo Province for second round hunt. It was about a five-and-a-half-hour drive there and the roads were great. We did have to pass through five tolls though. It was obvious that Joberg had grown a lot since 2007, when I was last here. We arrived at our new lodge, Olifantshoek, meaning elephant corner, that was surrounded by thick rocky mountains that look to be two or three thousand feet high. Also, this is a no poaching zone and from what they say, it means they can shoot to kill. We were greeted with charm and had a nice meal ready soon.

After our dinner, we drove about forty-five minutes to a blind where they had been baiting a spot with carcasses, fruits, piles of oranges etc. We sat up in the ground blind right at dark, all three of us. Deon has a real cool setup with motion sensors that would alert us if something approaches by vibrating his phone. The rifle has a small monitor on top of it and a piece that fits on the back of the scope. You do not look through the scope to shoot, you use the cross hairs in the monitor to shoot. I figured the motion sensors were going to be helpful because our heads were dropping dozing on and off. Quickly, a very full and beautiful moon was popping up through the blind window in just the right spot. Hour or so later, I saw a dik-dik. Then another one hour and a half or so a bird got my adrenaline going. Then a bit later, I saw an image out there and cut the scope on and swung the gun hard to the right, being careful not to bump or hit the blind. Softly woke up Deon and Tiffany, so they could see. Now the image is fine but not like looking through a scope. We made up our minds that it was a honey badger, something I had decided to add to my kill list, if we saw one. I was trying to get the crosshairs just at the shoulder area and steady the rifle, even though it was on a tripod. For a few seconds there, it seemed forever as the animal kept moving around and during that time frame, all the night sounds of Africa seemed to amplify making this a memorable moment for sure. So, I squeezed the trigger and it sounded like a hit. I saw it wheel and run off. I was happy and a bit sad because I would have rather seen it go down. Little later, we got out headlamps and found blood and started tracking out. Then sadly, after about 100 yards, it just quit. Despair started setting in but far from losing hope yet. So, we did the usual circles and zig zags looking. Finally gave in and Deon walked back to the truck and got JD. He set him up on the blood trail and he lit out, with a run on it. Chasing, we ended up at a big hole that I had just looked over at about a hundred yards past, where the blood trail had ended. He investigated it but took out in another direction. Luckily, he just made a big circle, I guessed, just double checking himself, and came back. So we let JD go in a bit more and could tell by the way he was acting that it was in there. Waiting a bit, Deon got down on his belly with the light and could see fur. He said, "Well it's an animal but not a honey badger". My heart kinda sank thinking I might have shot a baby leopard or something like that. Nope, he said it was a civet, one of the top three on my hit list! It was a nice mature one too. Happy, happy, happy, I was ole Italian redneck for sure.

DAY SIX

Woke up to lions roaring at sunlight. Here, they had about twenty-five acres of electrified high fence, surrounding the lodge that housed three rhinos. Outside of that there was about thirteen more acres of high fencing that held five full grown lions for protection. After breakfast, we spent a few hours riding around in search of a big male baboon. We see a lot of everything except a baboon, vermit monkeys, hippos, giraffes, warthogs, many birds, sables and much more roaming around and running all about.

Then we ended up moving our setup for tonight's hunt to a different spot. Another hunter had shot a Kudu the night before and did not find it until the next morning. The body showed a lot of sign of being eaten by a honey badger and hyena, so tonight that would be our new spot. They got the kudu out, so we're going to substitute it with my civet carcass and some kudu remains. All the meat here is eaten by people or other animals, nothing is wasted.

The night started out warm and still. It wasn't long, while the moon was not up yet, I cut on the scope light and seen a set of eyes, ended up being a bush pig boar. He spent a while scarfing down corn and left-over orange peelings etc. An hour or so later, Deon was out and so was JD, in Tiffany's chair. She sat it out tonight. A little later, saw a few more bush pigs and some impala. As the night passed, the wind increased and the temps dropped. It wasn't long before I found myself shaking like a leaf and my ass colder than a well digger's ass in Montana. So with five hours into it, I decided we might as well call it a night, we tried.

DAY EIGHT

Today was Sunday so we did not hunt but did go check baits and cameras. There had been some brown hyenas and baboons around. I did not have a permit for a hyena but I did hope to see some. I am after a baboon but they do not come out of the trees at night. Baboons will kill calves of other animals and cows as well and eat only the utter, leaving the rest to waste or to be eaten by scavengers. We decided to go for a ride and do something on Tiffany's bucket list, zip lining and I joined in. It was a lot of fun and had an awesome supper there too. Then we headed in for an hour nap or so before heading out for the night hunt.

We got out just at dark. We could tell something had been around because the bait pile was all dragged around. Looking at the tracks, it seemed to be warthogs and bush pigs. The night was perfect for the first few hours and in that time a civet and three bush pigs came out. One was a decent boar. Four more hours went by, the moon had risen well and it got pretty cold. We had heard a blue wildebeest blowing at us until Mother Nature called and I had to come out of the blind. They lit out like a bat out of hell. Our blind was half buried in the ground, so I figured they thought I was a monster at twenty-five yards, maybe. JD and me both got under blanket to keep warm. Finally, I convinced Deon I didn't think anything was going to move because it was too cold. He agreed so he stepped out to go to the truck and just like that he ran back in. He spotted something so we waited about thirty minutes. Sure enough a civet came back, but no honey badger.

DAY NINE

This morning was nice so we checked trail cameras at some bait sites, all the while looking for baboons. We could see tracks in the road now and then and even cut a leopard track, hoping to see it for sure. We decided on a bit of rest in a blind, by a watering hole, hunting before going back to the camp. A few hours at it, we had pleasure to see some beautiful dust devils/ mini tornado, spinning up dirt, dust and leaves into the air as the wind got stronger. One hit the blind forcing us to cover our faces and eyes like an attack. We also had a mother warthog come out for a while for a drink with two little ones, a nyala yearling, and some sables came out too. About that time, we heard a baboon in the distance giving me a little hope of seeing one. A little time went by and I caught a glimpse of what I thought was one but it ended up being a vermit monkey. He stopped at some 100 yards away from the watering hole. I figured he was scouting the area for safety for the rest of the troop which slowly moved up to meet him. Then he moved up cautiously but a bit wary. A few minutes later, another then another came out. There must have been forty scattered 300 yards throughout the back ground deep in the trees. Today I had the .300 Magnum so it was a little too small of a target to shoot. But I decided if I could get the bullet just right, I should be able to mount him. I took the chance and did well with a perfect lung shot behind the shoulder. It was a little rough on the other side but okay. Another amazing Africa critter down, full of teeth. These things are like our coons and opossums in the USA, they're everywhere and nowhere near extinction. They rob, destroy, and tear up all they can around farms, homes, and lodges all throughout Africa. This is the reason that some are hunted. I'm glad I got to take one and one is all I would ever want. Here in Africa, many farmers would just prefer to see them all dead, not all but most. By preserving it on a wall mount, I can show and share with the many folks back home, who will never be blessed, like me, to see them in the wild. By mounting it I hope to keep its memory alive somewhat for a while, like a picture but much better. It would be sad if one day all we had were pictures left.

For the evening hunt, we decided to drive a while and go to another farm where some farmers had killed some nuisance baboons and a brown hyena and had thrown out all the carcasses. We set up there to see if we can catch a honey badger coming in. All three of us are in a pop-up blind with blankets all set up for six hours or so. Before dark, two warthogs came in and fed on the carcasses. Later the sun fell behind the sky and it grew pitch black in the blind. I was staring at the stars through the little holes in the blind when the buzzer went off signaling us that something was at the bait. I then cut the infrared scope on and saw that it was just three bush pigs. Somewhere way off, we heard lions roar and a jackal cry. Then the sensor buzzed again, it was a big brown hyena. No permit so all I could do is sit and watch him tug and pull at the wired down carcass of one of his own, laying on the ground. It was easy to see his strength as it worked to tear the bait by lifting the large carcass of what may have been his brother or mother. Later, he came back for a second round. As the night grew colder and my butt grew weaker, sitting, I had had enough and was ready to say good night to the big sky in Africa and head in.

DAY TEN

We decided today if we didn't get a good sign of a honey badger we were going to sit for baboon in the evening. Then after eating and after dark we would get the spotlight and go out hunting for genet and white tail mongoose. Writing from camp, I get a glimpse of what looks like black impala. Hmm…

Now, before dark we decided to go after a big baboon at the Lekhale Zipline, property of Yohan, who had told us about the many baboons on his cattle farm. We got there early enough to scout a little bit and right in the middle of it heard one bark off in the distance heading our way. Now, a little rushed, we had to run and hide the truck and get back. Half way back across the mountain top we could see them scattering down the rocky thick mountain side, barking now and then, as if commanded by the pack leader. We got spotted and had to try to get a shot. It was difficult to try to keep up with the big male leader of the troop. Finding him and at what seemed to be the last chance before it got too thick. I had one shot, the way I seen it, so knelt down and laid my gun across a small broken tree, turned the scope up a bit and slung lead. There were some limbs, but I had to try. I've been wanting one big male my whole life, pretty bad. The way those things fly off the rocks, it was hard to say if I made a hit. Hard to hear as well with the dang wind at near 25 mph making the 357-yard shot even harder which was farther than I wanted to shoot. My original plan was to set up on the spot we figured they roosted and wait for them to come in. So, now we busted down the mountain and up the other side, looking for blood. Apparently, it was a miss though, so with only one light with us from the rush, we decided to go sit on the roost and see if they would still come in and they did. Interesting to say the least. There was a lot of barking, snarling and screaming going on from most likely fighting to see who got what tree and where. We were hidden too far back and it was dark now to see much with the naked eye. We could hear them all around us though, so we decided to sneak up on them and throw a light on them. When we did it sounded like a bomb went off all around us. I just hoped not to get scalped as they made a mad dash on their way out.

Drove back to camp and chowed down and me and Tiffany climbed in the back of the truck and went out into the bush shining for animals that only ever move at night. The first set of eyes we seen were brief and I think it was either a leopard or brown hyena. I had just seen the tracks in the sandy road too. Later, we found some bush babies, nocturnal primates with really big eyes. They bounce around a lot in the trees. We saw them a few times. Also, we saw a big hippo. Then we saw some eyes and with them also birds being forced out of the tree there. Deon, looking through binos, said. "genet", and with that word I leaped out the back of the truck and ran to the tree. With a lot of luck, it went up the tree instead of down to the ground. Instantly, I threw up the Benelli shotgun on the genet and pulled the trigger. It looked like I missed at first because it was just sitting still but actually it was just hanging there. I definitely did not want to shoot again and hurt the hide because I wanted to mount it. As it tumbled through the trees falling to the ground I ran to meet it, it was dead. I was very happy, for this was one of the animals on the top four I had hoped to see on this thirteen-day hunt. Beautiful to say the least. This one will be in my living room, in memory of it, for the rest of my living days. I do not care to ever shoot one again. This one is known as a cape genet, they are very common and far from being threatened. However, they can be a threat to poultry for sure but will also eat beetles, grasshoppers, crickets, seeds etc. Genets are considered omnivores. I guess, I was lucky we had a short night because we missed the cold.

DAY ELEVEN

This morning, waking up I was glad to see another hunter in the camp, from England, get the brown hyena we had seen the night before on our bait. Even though I couldn't shoot it because I didn't have a permit, which some animals require, I was just glad to see it up close. They have a head like a pitbull but bigger. We relaxed a bit and then headed to the canyon on the mountain to try to see baboons again, since we didn't have any pics on the camera. This seems to be the only area me and Deon can't agree on for the set up for the hunt. I'm more of an ambush hunter so it's hard for me to want to make long shots where they aren't needed.

Later, sure enough we hear barks in the distance and then black spots appear on the mountain side. First we see the scouts running up the tallest trees they could find now and then. Then a little later a big male came out. I stretched out the big .300 magnum and with my binos ranged him at 294 yards, lined him up in my cross hairs and squeezed off the shot with no luck it seemed. Then another opportunity came up at 359 yards and shot again but it was through a bit of small brush. After taking the shot, with my scope turned up and recoil with the big gun, I was lost to see anything. Deon was watching through the binos and was not sure. So he lit out down the canyon to go see while I spotted to direct him in the right direction if need be. There he finds blood. Hit was made but no animal. Later, he's back, exhausted, and says, "Get ready, they're coming back". Thirty minutes or so later, sure enough they did. Unfortunately, the best shot I had was 401 yards. We figured if I don't shoot I can't make a kill. However, I do not know the ballistics on this gun at that distance. Four hundred yards is farther than most think and I think a lot of hunters overestimate the ranges they shoot. Anyway, I leveled off the top of his head and sent lead flying but no luck. Very, very, sad dang day for sure. One of the downers during this trip so far, as my desperation grew stronger to get a big male baboon.

Back out after dark, we rode around shining and seen a good bit of game but nothing we were after. Everything we are looking for now, stays on the ground. The grass is very high here. It was good to see the hippos again out on range and a few bush babies and also an up-close encounter with an aardwolf to round the night off. It was the coldest night yet.

DAY TWELVE

Today we move to another lodge closer to where we will be hunting, for the last few days, the Chacma Lodge, owned by Win, who is a great guy by the way. Lodge is a fine place for sure. We settled in and then was met with a full spread for lunch. Then we headed out to a watering hole that had been baited earlier with lemons and oranges, in hope to see a big baboon. Randomly, throughout the day many different animals and birds came for a drink. Thanks to hunters there are now thousands of more watering holes in the bush than there ever was before. A lot of the Limpopo Province was once cattle farms now turned into hunting resorts. This is why there are more plains game than used to be in this area We saw one big boar warthog and by the time I convinced Deon to let Tiffany shoot it, it was gone. Probably good though because the shot might have spooked any baboons out of the area. The day was nice though, no wind and cool enough to sit in the blind with short sleeves and not get hot. There were other animals I would like to take but I'm about at the end of money on this trip for sure.

Back at dark, from day hunt, we ate a nice meal before heading out again. I must say that it is nice living in this short window of the rich, having your clothes washed, three meals cooked, coffee made, fire built for you and bed made up etc. All the lodges treated us right and more than met our expectations. The night was right to be in the back of the truck. We ran into a few genets and another civet. Also a lot of plains game as usual and one real nice sable bedded down. Then the bulb blew out on the spotlight but was lucky we had another. We got another good look at an aardvark too. Sometimes in the bigger herds, like impala, the eyes were so many it looked like Christmas lights. The African sights and sounds were all we took that night.

DAY THIRTEEN

After a good fruit and healthy cereal with coffee, we head to the blind for a sit until lunch. Perfect morning. Three nyala showed up and later a fourth big one came in and thought for a minute there was gonna be a fight. It was interesting to see how the hair on their manes on their backs and tails fluff up, in a fighting posture. A lot of wart hogs came and went. Got to see a few bristle up for a short fight. Plenty of birds were singing their tune all around.

We went back to the lodge to grab a good meal and dozed off in a big cushiony chair. Then scarfed down coke and headed back to the blind for the rest of the day. We weren't there long when a nice roan came out but was leery as could be. We also got entertained by a large troop of vermit monkeys. After we sat late, in the blind, we went back to the lodge to eat. It was after dark but we went to the pop-up blind to try to see some dang honey badger. Complete darkness grew fast and we all settled in. About every thirty minutes we added another layer of clothes on for a while. Soon, the buzzer went off, turned on night vision and saw a big sable standing there. Later on, a beautiful genet and then a brown hyena. We are told they are hard to see but since guess I can't shoot one, they seem to keep falling into my lap. We heard jackals a few times around us and was good to see the night stars. I think this is something we take for granted and lose by sleeping under roofs all the time. Hunting this way reminds me of so many around the world, war-stricken countries, homelessness and more, that don't even have the luxury right now of shelter. This might be my last night, so we stuck it out until 4 a.m. Nine hours. Eventually, just got really cold, even with a quilt. Ass died hours ago. We decided to head in for a warm bed. It didn't take much to feel blessed and I thanked Almighty God for another awesome cold ass night under the African sky. Mighty He is if you just have the faith it requires to see his blessing. Blessings like everything usually does not happen overnight.

DAY FOURTEEN (Chakma Baboon)

Slept in real late, but not real late so headed to the blind again. Right off vermit monkeys and a couple of nyala showed up to entertain us. A few birds came in after the orange peels Tiff had thrown out from the window of the blind and we saw warthogs off and on. Later, we heard the baboons barking in the distance. So my eyes glazed through dust, fallen leaves, rock and limbs for a black object. Maybe forty-five minutes later out of nowhere came the first big baboon. Five minutes later another then another. That was it for about twenty minutes. This is my third trip to Africa and baboon has always been first on my list, a male one. I shot a female in a rush through the rocks my first time hoping it was a male.

To my own shock, I must admit I was shaking. I think from wanting one so bad and the pressure of it being the last day also. Now my dilemma…was it a male or a female? They were all about a hundred yards. I was pretty convinced all were males but looking through the scope all the way up, I still could not see a penis or balls. Never thought I'd want to see them so bad. I had Tiffany looking through binos for the same things. I even had her, in a three-minute rush, google pics. I was so sure but no sign of goods had me feeling messed up. Then fifteen minutes or so later, some more started coming. Thank God I could plainly see these were males comparing them to the others. So now, I'm lining the crosshairs up waiting for the right shot. It felt like a day waiting on him to get in the right spot out from behind the tree etc., and stand right also. Good thing because it gave me enough time to calm down and get more mad than nervous. Finally, I squeezed the trigger and he lay dead in the spot I shot him. Though I still reloaded ready for anything. Walked up to him and rolled him over and could clearly see it was a male. He had a gnarly set of big teeth, torn nose and one eye out, clearly scarred up old warrior and leader of the troop. One anyone would want to take for sure. I'm definitely going to full body mount this ole guy. Such a relief for the last day's hunt.

We decide to try one more time for badger this last evening. After spooking a herd of blue wildebeests, we got settled in and got buzzed twice when a civit and then a group of bush pigs came in. One nice boar but no badger. So after four hours we decided to get back for some rest to go home. The longest flight is fourteen hours. It sunk in now that I would leave without a caracal or a honey badger but you can't always get everything. May be the good Lord will me another day.

CONCLUSION

Happy and blessed to have spent time again under the stars of the African sky. It would be such a terrible loss if these animals were not amongst us. The fact is without hunters most of these animals would not be. Even the game ranches and breeder ranches do so much for Africa's wild game. Spend ten days in the bush and you too will grow to love what Africa has to offer because there is not many other places that can compare to the experience that its wildlife will provide for the observer or the hunter. This world would not be the same without Africa, or anywhere for that matter. God don't make mistakes. What a day it will be when He returns and there will peace in heaven and Earth.

Chapter 18

MUSKIE TRIP WITH SUPER DAVE PINKERTON OHIO

This little trip just kinda came out of the spur of the moment by me and my step dad, Cullen Parker. On this trip, the goal was to slow life down a bit and spend time with my brother. He's always been my biggest inspiration, watching him conquering his limitations, being handicapped, and never ever complaining. He also had never flown in a plane, so I knew he would like it and he did.

DAY ONE

We met with good friends Scott and Steve, with hopes to share a boat with them in hopes of landing a trophy Muskie. But either way, I knew a good time and great memories was in store. Flights went well, smooth sailing. We got in our rental car, red Toyota Corolla race car and then lit out to Scott's. I was a bit excited to be there and see his trophy deer scoring up to 200 points. Arriving, he wasn't there so we quickly piled up for a short nap until he got off work.

Scott showed up and it was good to see an ole friend. Right off, we had to go to the trophy room to explore and share tales of some hunts gone by, a lot that only another hunter would understand. The trophy doesn't hang on a wall for just a memory of that kill but it gives honor to the animals and the challenge of the hunt. It sort of gives praise that it gave its life so that we can appreciate its life and the land it lives in and so much more.

So we decided right off to throw some nice steaks on the grill and while waiting yank some sheetrock off a wall and repair a water leak. That's what friends do now and then, pitch in and help. But it wasn't long before we were tying on to Scott's big Stratos boat with a 225 Mercury and heading out to Lake Plum Creek. Dragging and trolling four lines until midnight, for our first night there. It had turned oddly cold to say about 64 degrees and we think this sudden temp drop stopped any bites because we didn't even get one. However, it was fun being under God's big sky of stars together, sharing stories, cutting up a bit and having fun, David, Scott, Steve and me.

DAY TWO

Up and on our feet about 8:30 a.m., we finessed the coffeepot a bit and scarfed up a couple bowls of Cap n Crunch in some 2% milk and started a gang plan for another round of fishing. One of our plumbing repairs still needed addressing so after knocking that out we restocked the cooler and lit out. We was on the water just prior to dark after stopping at Auto Zone for a few new bulbs for the truck and boat to keep us from earning a big fat ticket. This time we put out six poles with four planer boards. After a few tangles and snaps we finally got lined out for some smooth runs. We did manage to snag a big log that had fallen over the edge of the lake shore. Again temps got down to two shirts and long pants it was a must. Not good. No bites. So about 1 a.m., we headed in to give our beds a long massage. We were plenty ready.

DAY THREE

We all decided that we were just going to have to man up and jump in the sun early today and see if that might change our luck. After a big chipotle burrito, we were all fuller than an opossum in a pumpkin patch.

Running four lines, we were blessed with a pretty flat lake. We started out along the shallow sides hoping something was there but spent too much time hung up in the grass, so we headed back to the deeper side and ran some deeper baits. After a few passes and a few miles, we heard that awesome sound of a line going out on a reel. Scrambling to snatch pole out of its holder, I managed to set the hook and bring in my first Saugeye fish. Happy as a bee in a sunflower field now. We ended up with four by night's end. It was a splendid night for sure. So, about 1 a.m., the Muskies have won again. Scott, is like me though, we don't quit so we'll try again tomorrow night, we hope.

DAY FOUR

Out of bed later than ever in years, at about 10 a.m., but with pleasure. The extra rest was nice for a change. It didn't take me long though, to heat water up in coffee pot. Watched a bit of TV, then got stirring, retying lines on reels and oiling them. We tried to get one trailer light back up as well. They're pretty proud of their parts with the prices they put on them. By now, we was ready to roll in some dough for food. Ended up at Squeaks Chance R, for about 45 wings. We stopped and fueled everything and couldn't help but grab an ice cream cone to finish making ourselves swollen with food for the night's fishing trip.

Made it out, a few hours before dark and went under the far bridge and tried some spots that Scott has never fished before, for an hour or so but no luck. Temps were rolling in at about 92 degrees with a slight wind. So off we go back towards the dam and deep side of the lake. The deepest we ran across was about 61 feet that we saw. With the sun going down and less traffic on this Saturday, and with about a thirty-to-thousand-dollar boat, we had a bit of anticipation, maybe for a hit. So trolling at three to four mph, it took a while to get from one side to the other. Hours later and about 11 p.m., I had dropped my chin and lost a good bit of faith even to the point that I pulled two rods in. Scott asked, "What yea doing?"

I said, "well we talked about stopping at 10 tonight, so think we gonna be beat on this one."

Nope, Scott don't quit, his mentality was still there. He says, "Heck no, we got to go a bit longer." I was just thinking maybe it was time as not to wear out my welcome. Boy was I glad we didn't ease out. At eleven one of the reels were singing that sound we had been hoping for where the drag was humming. Now trolling, they pretty much set hook themselves, so all we had to do was get rod tip up and keep it up and pray it stayed hooked for about 250 feet or so, up to the boat. We knew it was a Muskie from the feel of the rod. Kind of glad he wanted to stay down too. It didn't come up to for a head shake. Closer to the boat, it got easier to see that I may have trophy size representable fish to say I caught one. Sure enough it was worthy for a net and Scott was scrambling all the time while my butt was puckered tight with fear of losing this fish. As soon as I saw it in the net, it was like a pickup truck had been lifted off my back. Yelp, nice one! Scott was excited as I was and in our final hour to get it done. Happy, happy, happy. My first Muskie and thirty-eight inches long. Worthy for sure to put a pic on the wall. I did not choose to mount it, but was worried at first that I might not have no choice because the fish wanted to float on its side while trying to release it. So, we grabbed it, pulling it back and forth making water pass through its gills, in hope it regained strength after the stress we put it through. The hot temps of the surface water didn't help either. We were lucky though, and managed to watch him swim into the deep with a spot light. So our encounter was full circle after about thirty-five to forty hours of just trolling.

Now, it kinda sounds nuts for just one fish, but one is better than none when it is something you set out to accomplish for a hunting trip. Same as life. Sometimes yea just can't stop. Never give up, rough the ups and downs and keep plugging along. But the master plan is to always have faith through Christ Jesus and yourself. So, after a little visit at Steve's house, Scott's twin, we hurried back to clean up a bit and relish our victory in our minds but with our back and butts flat against a nice comfy mattress.

DAY FIVE

Wow second latest sleep-in years! We was up scarfing down coffee and peanut butter sandwiches and discussing days gone by. Then we put away all the fishing gear and got ready for freeway meal tonight, before this journey ends and we head back to Louisiana, David Parker and I. Mission accomplished with great memories.

Chapter 19

BACK ACROSS THE BORDER TO MEXICO

DAY ONE

This trip started the day after Christmas with me rearing to see it over so I could go. On the road through Houston, which is never good, I was on my way back across the border, to the Violin Ranch and the one I named High 6 near Paras and Guerrero.

December 26th at about 4:30 a.m., and I lit out for the 550 mile or so drive, about nine or ten hours. We were blessed with nice weather all the way. I grew tired about the seven-hour mark and had to scarf up more coffee. We got there in time to half ass unpack and grab our bows. The rifles were not there yet, we thought we would find out later. Before getting here, we had a militia encounter, where the farm road meets the highway. They let us pass but not without a lot of questions, of course. It's a little intimidating with AR's and 50 Cals pointing at you. We also stopped at the drive thru liquor store in Paras and grabbed up some corn. We got my buddy spreader hooked to the receiver on my truck, filled it with corn and lit out.

Since, I was armed with a bow, I decided to get up in a cut off road, backing my chair up in the cactuses and using two big pads to help me get high enough, for a better shooting position. After parking my truck, hidden, about 150 yards away, I rushed to my stand, sat down, strapped binos on, ranged the area with the range finder and sprayed a little cover up scent on. It wasn't five minutes later, I heard hoof steps close to my right coming through the rocky terrain. Out steps the first deer, a big doe and then a yearling. Seconds later another doe and before long seven does and one yearling were out in front of me. Then like a ghost, a seven-point pops out taking control of the main area, to get his share of the corn. Nice buck but not nice enough yet. Soon, a smaller buck came out chasing a doe. Then, like someone threw a bomb in the middle of them, they all lit out in a run. Seconds later, eleven dang shoat pigs showed up scrabbling for corn like they had never eaten before. They fed there about twenty yards out. I drew my bow and shot one of them, about sixty pounds, laying him in his tracks. The rest of them scrambled off and a bit later a few deer came back, but no shooter. Dark now falling, so I grabbed my hog and headed to the truck to make my way back. The Mexican living at the ranch took the pig. Never got his name, he didn't speak a lick of English and I didn't speak a lick of Spanish. For the evening hunt Jared and I both saw small bucks and does.

DAY TWO

This morning, I go to a different spot and it wasn't long before I hear crunching of corn just where I had put corn but could not see it. Patiently waiting and bow standing ready, I was happy and sad I seen it, a javelina. First one and then four more appeared. Nice male about twenty yards out, so I drew my bow and slung an arrow into him. With a long howl of a squeal, he bolted out into nearby cactus. Haveys, short for javelina, went everywhere. Soon after, a spike and three does came out and about twenty minutes later a huge flock of blackbirds descended on the scene and spooked all the deer off. Closer to dark, a yote, coyote, came by but not close enough for a shot.

Back to camp, for a mid-morning breakfast, Robbie Warner and William Ennenbach had showed up. So as soon as they unpacked, we drove out to show them a few places for a first hunt. On the way in, we are reminded of what lurks in this country, a rattlesnake was in the road. I stomped his head good.

For the evening hunt, I got set up along a fence row and was floored by amount of deer that came out. I'm guessing it was between nine and thirteen, in and out of the road. I now had a 30.06 bolt action rifle. One nice chocolate horned high eight point fed for the longest time. One havey and its baby passed in front of me at only five yards. She wasn't happy, snapping her jaws at me with her hair raised. I sat still and she went on. Haveys are interesting creatures for sure, with large teeth, and very fast also. Like hogs at home, they don't seem to see very well without movement. William had success this evening and took his first Old Mexico whitetail deer, being a nice wide six point.

DAY THREE

Up and out warming the truck at 5 a.m., cranking the generator and loading the coffee pot, I sucked down a peanut butter and honey sandwich. It was a perfect 45-degree morning. Got my corn out a bit early and before the sun rose I saw a dark image appear in the road, about 125 yards down, and I could hear the corn getting snapped. Ducks flew above me headed to the lakes on the ranch. Then all the deer just kind of busted up, and out in the road jumped a high rack nine-point chasing after one of the does. He went running by me a few times at twenty yards. Unfortunately, the morning passed with no big shooters showing up. It warmed up fast, so packed up and drove around the ranch, scouting spots and now and then looking for arrow heads.

After lunch and a nap, we headed back out and got Jared set up. I wasn't in my stand long before I realized that I had gotten a few small cactus burs in my left thumb. Talk about aggravating. It wasn't long before I had a deer on one end of my lane and deer on the other end. One decent eight point and a five point were out with does. I had to laugh when an inattentive yearling came close to getting into my lap. Just before sundown, I decided to check my rifle, dropping a havey at about 120 yards which helped to boost my confidence in the rifle. I did fire a few shots earlier, at the ranch, at some targets that were set up. That is always a must before hunting.

DAY FOUR

Well the night got interesting, about 2:15 a.m., the militia stormed in our sleeping quarters with AR-15s and flashlights shining at the boys. It was just a check but spooky for sure. They were hunting cartel boys. However, they worry me as much as the cartel does, sometimes. What made it even more crazy, is that they never came into my room and somehow I slept through all of it! We ran out of corn yesterday evening. There was some left but I let Robbie and them use it, so I slept in. Later, Scott, owner of Mexico Hunting, brought about fifteen bags.

So, we all went back out at about 11:30 a.m. for the rest of the day, after giving the camp a massive cleaning. I decided to hunt in a stand we call the Coon stand, by one of the lakes. The weather had kinda gone to crap, high winds and a misty cold rain. So, it made getting in the box easy. It wasn't long a dozen does or so popped out a little at a time. Then a six point and a spike hassled a young doe. I don't think the rut was on but close. These young bucks in their first year, just don't know, not really, if a doe is ready yet. I got a glimpse of a big buck at about 500 yards or more crossing the road, kinda limping.

As dark grew closer, out popped a large bodied deer. Quickly, I put my binos on him and my heart began to race a little more, as I looked him over at different angles. I was thankful for having the time to do that. Now, I was hoping to see something step out, that the second I saw it there wouldn't be any doubt. So, the more I looked, the more I saw that he was nice enough. I turned my scope up to six power, laid it across my coat in the stand, steadied my rifle and put the cross hairs on his shoulder, hoping to take out some of his running gear so

I won't have to chase him through the cactus. Then I squeezed off the shot and he bolted. Feeling confident, from the high kick he made, from a decent ethical shot, I waited thirty minutes or so before finding my ten-point buck about 115 yards from where I hit him. It's always good to have a quick kill. Robbie took his first havey ever.

DAY FIVE

Still nasty weather, I decided to try to see if I could find the big limping buck that I had seen the other morning. I had gotten out early enough to use my cutters to nip a hole out in a cluster of cactus and brush. All a long being sure no snakes ended up in my lap, while I sat and waited on ole limp buck. I sat right in the spot he had crossed, hoping for luck. I also scattered a whole bag of corn, at 125 yards, in hopes to draw out deer that in turn will draw him out as well. Amazingly, as quick as I sat down deer were coming out from every direction. The corn here has something added to it that has an amazingly strong smell. It's all low fence and no one feeds here all year. It seems these deer just don't see and smell fear from humans like most places in the world that I've hunted. I think that some or even most have never seen a person. One of the last wild frontiers left in the world, I think. Soon, very surprisingly, there was antlers everywhere, ending up being nine bucks with two nice shooters out. Does getting chased, bucks pushing each other and does fighting, everything going on at once. Crazy! Time was creeping by. I figured surely, limp buck would show. Then at the edge pops out a big ten point with curled horns, which was hard to pass up but he didn't stay long. As fast as the hooked ten point popped out he lit out because in came ole limp buck. He walked right behind a clump of cactus. Now as the seconds went by, my adrenaline started to fly. I wanted this buck. He was a wide big bodied mature deer. Then he disappeared running a smaller buck off. It felt like my heart fell out of my chest. At that time a nice eight point walked out at thirty yards and starts tearing up a tree. Watching him, I calm just a bit and out of the corner of my eye, limp buck steps back out and this time in the wide open. It didn't take me long to get him in my scope and pull the trigger. I didn't really see a kick, so I was a little worried. I waited long enough for most of the deer to dwindle away before going to look, only spooking a few does and a small buck along the way. There wasn't much blood at the actual spot where I shot him but at about ten yards I found blood. Not too excited yet, moving along slowly through cactus, ready to shoot if need to, looking for more blood and thicker. Wasn't much longer, at about 100 yards, he laid. At first glance, I was very satisfied. I had taken a warrior. Antlers wide enough that one ear wouldn't hardly touch the ground. Soon, I saw where there was a hole in the joint of his leg, either from a bullet or from fighting. It was festered up pretty bad. The buck ended up twenty-three inches wide and scored second place in the wide division in Freer, Texas.

Out a little earlier than usual this evening, I was watching a covey of quail hustling up some corn that I had put out. Now and then, a rat would run out for its share and spook them a bit. Then like a bomb went off, a flock of about hundred black birds descended on the ground and the quail lit out. Later on, two does and a yearling came out but it wasn't long before seven shoats came and pushed them down the road. One lonely spike eased his way to the corn as I slowly watched the daylight turn to dark, with the dark came New Year's Eve. I finished off that day in bed by 8:30.

DAY SIX

This morning was perfect at about forty-five degrees. I took Robbie with me and sat him down, where I had taken the limp buck. I went curled up in some brush down the road, by the lake after spreading some corn out at about one hundred yards away. I barely got to sit down before deer popped out. Some deer even walked ten yards by me. I could hear their hooves first coming down the road. Before long, I had eleven does and yearlings and one 110-inch buck and another about 130 inches. (This is a way of measuring antlers)Then I was startled when Robbie shot. The deer just looked up. Another thirty minutes went by and another shot. Finished up with some beautiful bird sightings and a dog fight which made for a great morning. Back to pick up Robbie, it was easy to see that he was happy. We discussed his morning and then started to track his deer. It ended up being a very nice buck.

The evening was chilly but not cold just a bit windy. So decided to hunt a spot off the beaten path after setting out Jared. He is a new friend I made renting from me, who has always dreamed of making a hunt away from home, so we done the best we can to help him. As the sun fell and the wind calmed, a doe and young yearling popped out from the cactus like ghosts at about twenty yards. The yearling was small and curious, with me probably being the first human it has ever seen, it came within ten yards of me. They weren't there long when they threw their heads up looking back into the brush. About that same time, I heard grunting every minute for five minutes plus. What walked out was a shock but was not as well. I knew a pig was coming but a three legged one was unexpected. Watching this hog maneuver was odd and I kinda felt sorry for it. But the hog problem is real all over, so, I ended her struggle. About the same time, I heard Jared shoot. He got his second buck, a nice main frame eight point. Also, he had taken an ole havey, we've seen a lot, named club foot. She was also a cripple. Two in the same day, I was feeling kinda sorry for them.

DAY SEVEN

I began to grow a bit tired for lack of rest and the weather was terrible, so I figured it was a good day to sleep in a bit. I decided to go to Paras to gas up and get a bit of groceries.

Since I missed the morning hunt, I decided to get in the chair early. It was pretty windy. I sat in one spot for about an hour and then moved over to another spot. I didn't see a single deer but I did shoot a 200-pound sow to feed the stinking coyotes and buzzards. Robbie ended getting his best deer, a ten-point making three down. I did find a nice arrowhead in an old lake bed. Crazy thing was when I picked up Jared while he was walking to the truck, I saw him bend over and raise up quickly with his hands in the air and a happy face. He found one too, his first one! Very happy! Jared had also seen a lot of deer this evening.

DAY EIGHT

After a bit of sleep, I left out early and decided to make the half hour drive to what we call the High 1000 ranch, alone. Robbie and

Jared were leaving mid-morning headed back home, leaving me alone in Mexico.

So before daylight, I set up my pop-up blind in a spot that I had hunted last year. I wasn't really wanting to shoot any pigs but after they came and gone a few times, a multi colored pig stepped out and I dropped the hammer on that one. I never saw a deer, so I decided to make a loop around the ranch scouting and looking for arrow heads along the way. It was easy to see that the deer were not here like in the previous years and I was betting it was because the hogs seemed to have taken the area over. I was a bit nervous though, enough that I wasn't really having a good time because the cartel was using the road through this ranch a lot. I figured my truck and everything else would be a nice take for them and probably my life with it. I stayed until dark and saw one small buck and a doe.

So, I get back to the ranch and walk into the little room I was staying in and all my stuff is gone. Turns out the guy working there moved all my stuff to the main bunk house. I was not happy at all. Everything was all out of place and had gotten dirty. To make things worse, my new cot and bed roll were gone as well as all the mattresses from the main bunk house. Scott had sent some guys to get them and in the process they took my stuff too. Very pissed! Also, the deer head that I had brought to the owner, as a trade, was on the floor of the cook room all busted up. Now, I had to decide to sleep in my truck or drive the hour to Guerrero, at night, pack all my stuff and stay at the house Scott had just gotten. I didn't want to be on the highway that late but did. I got in town about 11 p.m. and ended up staying in the new house. But it was rough, for a country boy, because of all the dogs going at it all night. So frustrated, I drove back out to the ranch got my gear, payed Scott, hid the gun in the woods and headed home. It's a long drive with no sleep, but was a great memorable hunt. I love it down there but could do without the uncertainty though. It is a sad situation. I ended up stopping in Freer Texas to see where everyone was at in the Muy Grande contest. My wide glide ended up second in place for the whole division in Mexico. So, in conclusion I tolerated the nine plus hour drive home and was glad to be there.

Chapter 20
LOST AS KIDS

So one time me and my cousin Frank Brunix decided to fish Calcasieu River by my grandma Edith Williams. Back then, us like many would go out with a gallon of gas, back when it was cheap, rake some leaves back and "gas" some worms to use for bait, first. It was always a game to see who got the longest ones. Some would be twelve plus inches or more.

Off we went and one thing led to another, each trusting the other until we were lost which was a rare thing for us. We had covered miles and in them days there wasn't much traffic so it didn't help to listen for a car so we could go to the road. We finally ended up about eight miles away on the wrong highway. So mean time while they were looking for us, in the woods, they were hollering "Booger, booger", because that was Frank's nickname. Well in the South a booger can mean a ghost, boogeyman or pretty much anything frightening. So hearing them all calling booger through the woods, some people off a farm came out with guns looking for the Booger! Funny Stuff!

Chapter 21
OPENING DAY TURKEY SEASON 2019

Double up with Tiffany

S o this morning started at 5:30 a.m. with the usual waffle covered in peanut butter, chocolate, almonds, syrup and honey and a strong cup of coffee. Then out the door with my lady Tiffany Edwards, the love of my life. It's always good to share hunts with those you love. I had gone out the evening before and spotted this bird and it was kinda late, so I felt good that he had roosted there somewhere close. After soaking up Deep Woods Off mosquito spray for the third time, we finally stopped looking like we was fighting ourselves slapping them off. We then got settled in, now good enough to see good in every direction. I let out the first yelp on my slate call. Kinda to my shock immediately there was an answer from a hen. She flew down the road right to my decoys and started clucking and yelping like a mad woman that had just baked a cake and it fell or something. She paraded back and forth ten yards in front of us. Both of us were doing all we could to be very still to not spook her off, knowing that this was the best decoy a turkey hunter could ever have. Then, to my surprise we heard what sounded like a gobble a hundred yards away. You see the LDWF, Louisiana Department of Wildlife and Fisheries, set the opening season date way back. This caused a lot of folks to get fired up because they felt that the hot time for chasing hens was gone. Nevertheless every now and then, and closer and closer a bird would gobble. Soon, I saw a blue head eighty yards out, through trees. Then sixty yards out and that is where he hung up, behind the ditch line and where Tiffany could not see him. She was the primary shooter this morning. I didn't even have a gun in hand. Then looking closer, I realized there were two gobblers. Things just got interesting and I was excited to see how this played out. Time kept ticking away and Tiff was growing weary with heavy arms, holding my Berretta ready for a shot. Finally, here they come and to my happiness both mature long beard toms. One was in full strut and the other falling right behind him. Now twenty-five yards, if that, I whisper to Tiff, "don't take all day, take the one in back," it looked the biggest. Ka wom, the gun rang out and now on the ground and turkey flopping. I grabbed the gun in midair, because it had flung out of my girls hands when she shot, and lucked up to get a shot on the second bird and then another to make sure it was down. We doubled up to make a memorable morning!

Three and a half number two shot had stomped my lady a bit with a big rosy spot on her cheek. I felt kinda bad and thought I should have used a little lighter load. Nevertheless, she's tough and we both are very happy. Her bird had a nine-and-a-half-inch beard and mine had a ten-and-a-half-inch beard. A lot of blessings of meat, with no doubt from the good man above. Turkey hunting is a special sport, with the excitement of the battle. Unfortunately, at this time I fear a big setback in the turkey population around here with the increase of hogs. It's flat-out miracle that any turkeys survive with 95 percent of the nest compromised by fire ants, coons, hogs and all other critters. And when they hatch they are as small as chicken bitty. Without human intervention I'm pretty sure they would not make it in most states. God blessed us to be blessed by the critters and all forest and land they dwell in and it is most definitely worth fighting to keep and protect. Probably more so than most anything on earth.

Chapter 22
RIO TURKEY HUNT TEXAS 2019

This hunt started out by coming through a real bad storm in Houston, heading to Victoria and DeWitt County to meet up with Alan, Dustin and Earnest. Robbie decided to ride along for the hunt. We got there about 3 pm, and started setting up our tents. We threw on our turkey vests, grabbed decoys and headed to the woods. Didn't see a lot of sign right off but didn't expect to from the rain. Rain had stopped about six hours ago, so I decided to keep walking until maybe we see some tracks. I hit the call every now and then trying to get a gobble out of one. It was still windy and cloudy and the temps were rising.

At about two hours before dark, on an old road, I spotted a blue head walking to the woods. We sat still a bit then scrambled to locate a good spot for both of us to sit together if we could. Sometimes that's hard. Ended up in a small cluster of oaks tucked up into brush. I set my funky chicken decoy and my pretty girl hen up. Got locked in my chair, took the safety off of my Berretta twelve gauge loaded with three- and half-inch number five load, strapped my padded knee rest on and broke out my slate call and ran a striker across it, Yelp, yelp, yelp. Right off, we both got that look a kid gets when he sees a Christmas present he always wanted, when gobbles rang out at what sounded like 150 yards, in front of us. Now, we had flipped a quarter for who gets to shoot first and I won. Now, my slate call let out a few more clucks, purrs and yelps and we hear a gobble again. Now closer, we know they are committed. At this point, we both raise our guns to our shoulders and then all of a sudden there they were at twenty-five yards. They were locked on and strutting in to the decoys in full splendor and beauty. Twenty-five yards is close enough to feel the vibration from when they drum. Everything you hope to see in spring turkey hunt is happening now and two gobblers at that. So with a whisper, I told Robbie that I would take the one on the right and for him to take the one on the left. But not before we watched them beat up decoys, gobble and even considered the kill because they were a little small. They weren't jakes, so we decided it was a good start. One, two, three, bam, bam and then bam again with me having to shoot twice. Somehow, some way, I had lost the front sight off my gun. All I could do was blame it on that. Both birds down and a double with a friend couldn't be bad. On top of that just yesterday morning, I did it with my girl Tiffany too! Wow! My bird sported about a seven- and half-inch beard and Robbie's about six. We figured it was a good start and still was plenty enough leg meat to make a good meal and breast meat to fry a few pieces, also.

Great memory for two friends struggling in our older years trying to enjoy the great outdoors. Just being out in Dewitt county and surrounding areas is a blessing this time of year. Everything green, flowers abound and sound of bees everywhere doing their thing. God bless the bees. Butterflies are all over and even the spiders are out and about to add to the beauty. Nighttime at camp near the Guadalupe River is lit up in some places by the fireflies. Every day in this environment, I feel the presence of my God, who I give all the glory to his design.

The next morning, sleeping through a cool night, we headed out to the two hundred fifty acres, Mr. Ernest has, for the first time. We heard one gobble now and then way off. Being the only one, we knew we had to muster up more of the "want to" and go. We had to cross a barb wire fence and when Robbie stepped on the bottom wire, the staple came out letting the fence drop and the top wire of bob wire about interfered with his family jewels. Not good. All was okay but it could have been bad. So now the chase is on and we already went a mile and it kind of seemed like he was running from us instead of to us. But we kept heading in his direction when he would give us a rare gobble. About the time we thought he was done and stopped gobbling, I hit the call and we heard a double gobble that sounded seventy-five yards off. So we had to just jump in the bushes pretty much. I could tell he was committed. It was Robbie's turn to shoot so I'm calling and his gun is ready. Sure enough, I see him down the road running and stopped just shy one step before he would have seen us. Robbie slung lead but with no luck. So now, ole happy, sad time.

Now, on the way back, I decided to make a big loop back and down by the river. I hit my slate call and one gobble, close. Same scenario, we were strapping on face masks, setting decoys, scrambling for a tree to plop down by and more. After all that, I gave a cluck and a cackle and again a gobble. He was coming. Sure enough ended up about twenty-five yards out. He stopped and started to throw his head up. It was easy to see that he was a mature shooter with full round tail feathers and a long beard. I would have loved to have a few more yards out in the wide open, but it wasn't gonna happen. So, I exploded the shell at him and he went down flopping. I bolted up ready for round two if need be but it wasn't necessary. It ended up being my best Rio I ever took, I think. He was easy twenty-eight pounds, inch and a quarter spurs and a twelve-inch beard. I was happy as a dog off the chain, strutting around there myself.

Later, the day had warmed up enough that relaxing in the tent was rough in the heat. So, we ended out early walking and calling. After making a large loop, we ended up back at camp. Our intention was to still go back and with about two hours left of daylight, while sitting at camp, we heard a gobble, so we didn't stay long. Scarfing down a water bottle and a candy bar, we lit out and were set up. A lot faster than we wished for a bird appeared fifteen yards from us and Robbie slung lead. Crap, clean miss! Bird was gone and we were shocked. Robbie was pissed. Ten minutes later another gobble. Shocked, we sat right back up, almost in the same spot. There he came, ole white, red and blue head bobbing straight and slinging gobbles, to keep us on high alert. Then bang at twenty yards. Dang another clean miss! Now, I was aggravated and Robbie done got so pissed that he slung his gun through the woods. Hee-hee. Well, ended up that he just bought a new choke and something was wrong with it. A few hours later, it actually ended up being pretty funny for us. Nevertheless, it was good times and good memories, Thanks Robbie for the company.

Chapter 23
BEAR HUNT ARKANSAS 2021

Hello, this story started out really in 2019. I had seen a place for sale in the Ozarks and I had been looking for an excuse to just go somewhere so we went to look it over. I ended up on Hwy 65 in Western Grove Arkansas, about twenty miles from Harrison. Seven miles off of the highway I ended up buying ten acres that meets the national park with the Buffalo River in site at the bottom of the mountain. It is just a beautiful place full of hardwoods and rocky out crops. Within a year, I had a cabin built that was pretty close to what I have always dreamed of. I also, got my stands and feeders set up for deer season.

So, my second day of the first season when I was just deer hunting, a small bear passed me. I knew there were black bear but I wasn't really thinking to hunt them. However, I decided why not give it a shot. So, the second season, I prepped for them and ended up short after raising my box stand building and deck, from about a 45-degree slope. Doing this, changed a lot of my sight paths with trees and limbs so I could not get a shot on him. Unfortunately, that was the only bear that came out. A lot of acorns had fallen that year, so they were not moving all over.

Now fast forward to 2021. I left four days early before bear season opened. I stopped by the grocery store, on the way up, and bought sardines, tuna, dog food, marshmallows, box of cereal and some cheap cookies. I added all of it to the frozen bag of fish heads and guts I had been saving from fishing. When I got to my land, I hung all of it from a tree that I had bent over to get it in the air. Checking my deer cams, I had bears on everyone and everywhere. I was also getting them at a bait site where I had paid a neighbor, to throw out a few sacks of dog food once a week for three weeks. You are allowed to bait 30 days before opening day. I had to do this because Hicks, Louisiana is about six plus hours away.

Now two evenings before the season began, I just went to sit and both days up to four bears came, a sow with two big cubs, that were about grown enough that their mother was about ready to force them off, and one other. It was fun just to watch and video and also made my confidence high in taking one this year. On the last evening, on my out, I threw out more cookies, marshmallows, and an open can of sardines that I hung high from a limb.

Up at the cabin, with the night cool enough I built a fire. I decided to keep it simple and just use some kerosene lamps as not to raise any noise since my box stand and bait were only 170 yards down the mountain. This night I warmed up some soup on the woodstove since the fire was already hot in it. Sleeping, off and on, filled with over anxiousness for the next morning, I was up two hours before daylight drinking a cup of good ole swamp coffee. I toasted up some bread on a black iron flat skillet and ate toast with peanut butter and honey.

Now down the mountain, quiet as a mouse and in my box sitting in the pitch black, I hoped for the best. It was an awesome morning, crisp and cool with squirrels all about and the birds singing. My Raven crossbow was between my legs and propped up on the window. I pulled out my range finder just to double and triple check the yardage all around. Never make a shot you are not sure of. After having to about come out and beat some squirrels chasing each other and making a ton of racket on top of my stand, like a ghost one cub appeared 15 yards, coming out from the ravine and then the other. It took a bit longer for the momma to show. They all ended up laying down eating what they could find. Stretching my head while watching them to make sure the cubs were big enough to be on their own, I had no doubt they were. After they all milled around a bit, all of a sudden something spooked them and they all ran up a tree. I figured it was a boar coming and one that I hoped to see. They didn't stay up in the trees too long and I never say a thing. Back down on the ground they continued picking up scraps around the site where I had thrown out bait. The big sow ended up dead on a 30-yard spot. So I leveled off my Raven cross bow and got it steady on the window of my box stand, made quick prayer and pulled the trigger. She spun, growled and ran to the top of the hill and then fell where I could just barely see a spot of black. Sitting for a couple of minutes, thinking she may move, I got reloaded and started the stalk. I do not like any animal that has given its life for mine to suffer even for a second. I would rather take a chance of getting ate up from a charge to finish the animal than not try at all. Within 15 yards in hole of mountain rock, I saw her and she did move, so I shot again. I wasn't even gonna think about the chance of this thing getting down the mountain and losing her. I sat and watched her until she kind of rolled over then went and looked. She was bigger and older than I thought judging by a yellow chipped tooth in her head. It's now 70 degrees and it would be a couple of hours until Mark would be coming so no time to dolly around. I had to get this big thing skinned and on ice fast. Bear will spoil faster than pig, pretty much.

My plan was to try and smoke a deer after I had bear hunted and I felt blessed to get on with it. With really nowhere to keep this much meat in the heat and the period of time I still had left hunting between Oklahoma and Arkansas so I called one of my many friends that I made here, for some help. Brian brought me some ice and lent a hand skinning and was glad to take the meat off my hands. He was more than happy for the meat and said it would be just right for a cook out with his biker club. I did keep the back straps and ate some on the second night. It was about all my propane icebox would freeze. Skinning the bear was a bit of a task since she was flat on the ground at a forty-degree angle. Big girl was plenty fat for sure. I caped her out for a full shoulder mount and kept the claws. I decided on the shoulder mount because I already have a full body mounted black bear from Alaska.

Afterwards, I had to call my bear in and report my kill but their system wouldn't be up and running for another five days. I also had to send a premolar in within seven days of the kill to the state. I was very thankful to the Lord above that I was one of the 500 people that got a bear to help the state keep the population in check.

Bears area beautiful and interesting animals but can become a nuisance tearing up cameras, feeders, cabins and more. The bear is mounted and hanging in my home now.

Chapter 24
SNIPE HUNTING

So this story is one that many young folk, in the South, have most likely experienced. Adults would take the young kids in the family out in the woods with paper bags, when we still had them, and then set each one of them alone, in different places, in the pitch dark. They would tell them to sit still and wait until they heard a snipe go into the paper bag then close it up. Now, this was never gonna happen so it was more a test of courage, I guess yea could say. It was kinda a test to see who had it in them, to see if they were brave enough to sit the entire time before the adults came back for them.

Now one Thanksgiving night, my dad and uncles decided it was time to take us kids, me, my cousin Frank and my buddy Mike, while my grandmother, Edith Williams, mother and my aunts were quilting in the spare room. Remembering the best I can, we was about ten years old at the time. They sat us down one at a time here and there down the old tram on Calcasieu swamp. After a good while I knew something was not right. Now even at ten years old, I had already been all over them woods playing so I was not completely lost for long. I went to fetch the other boys and we were all kind of confused, so I took us all back in the dark, back to grandmas. When we walked in the house alone we were asked were all the men were. The gig was up and "them mommas were madder than a wet hen", that the men had played a rotten trick on us boys and had left us alone in the woods. So they decided to turn the tide and we all waited until they came back much later. Now, when the men came back, to check to see if we were there, momma told us all to hide. The ladies told them that we weren't there and were very upset at them for leaving us. Well now even more worried, they went back for hours looking for us in a panic. I'm not sure who got the better of who at the end of it all. But boy, we was on the bad list the next day! We didn't even go squirrel hunting with dogs like we usually do. Ha! Ha!

Chapter 25
DUCK AND DOVE HUNT MEXICO

S ince, I wasn't getting to duck or dove hunt like I would like to, I decided to put together a little hunt. So, I called my ole buddy Don Mc Kenis. He'd been to this place before and figured he would be good help. Hank Stephens fell in with us too. We decided to cut out at about 11 p.m., meeting up at a super market in town. We had just been through a record-breaking freeze, so we were excited to go. The trip down was rough but the conversation catching up, from time gone by, made the eight hour drive a little better. It was a comfortable ride in my new Ford Raptor.

DAY ONE

We arrived about 8 a.m., at the Laredo Airport where I would be leaving my truck in long term parking. There we met Richard, the outfitter. We picked up a few groceries and other supplies and headed to the border. We got called over and went through the inspection with our gear etc. Afterwards, we went to get a visa and drove about one and half hours to Sabinas Hidalgo, to the lodge and got set up. Then scarfed up some lunch. Tired as we were, we still opted to head out to make an evening hunt. Started out slow but sped up at dark with a nice shoot. Supper couldn't come soon enough, we had chili rellenos. Man, it was great and I overate and felt like a pregnant armadillo.

DAY TWO

Off our asses and on our feet at about 4:30 a.m., anxious and ready, we headed to the duck pond. We threw out about forty decoys and before we could see the end of a barrel, ducks were hitting us in the face. Soon it was on along laughs and good fun. We were dropping ducks in every direction. Of course joking around, I had to make it out like I was the only one that killed all thirty-six of the ducks downed. Black mallards, gadwalls and a cinnamon teal put the icing on the cake. Also, taken were ringnecks, and blue and green wing teals and wigeons, which are pretty hard to come by they said. The hunt lasted to about 10 a.m. It didn't hurt to have Stacey Richard's pit bull retrieve the ducks.

After lunch and a quick siesta, we were headed back to the small lake. I decided to sit on the other side, in hopes to keep the ducks moving back and forth. It wasn't long before a few shells were ringing and I heard a few birds slamming into the water to their dying death. Now and then, we take a few just as they hit the water. It was a decent shoot but not phenomenal. One time I took a pop shot at a fast-flying duck straight over my head, before I knew it I was flat on my back. The bird boy, Marcel, got a good laugh out of it.

DAY THREE

In the truck after a cup of swamp water and grabbing a few burritos for a mid-morning breakfast we headed to a new pond. We ended up with a few birds, but it was real, real slow. Moon was full so we assumed the ducks fed a lot at night early. We did have a huge coon come out and walk the levee where we were sitting, to see what all the commotion was about. Later in the morning, I made a long walk and ended up finding a few arrowheads to make my day.

That evening, Don and Hank went to try to get Hank a javelina and I went back to sit at the pond. So, I threw out a few decoys and got settled. About twenty minutes into it, I heard that familiar sound of a loud swoosh and in came a duck cupping up to land. Bang! Bang, one duck down. Then a big boar hog walks out too far to shoot. Of course, I doubt 7 1/ 2-inch bird shot would have done anything other than make him mad. Then to my surprise, I was just glaring into a tree and seen a big coon, in the forked branches, watching me it seemed. Big Coon. I decided if I could reach him across the pond with this Beretta 12 gauge, I would take him to mount. Bang, bang, bang! No luck he just walked down the tree and disappeared. I ended up popping one blue wing teal and cut out. They did not get any javelina.

We cleaned up and packed up and settled in for a death-defying drive home through the border. All the way, I'm remembering a short yet memorable trip. They don't have to be long to keep and hold good memories.

Chapter 26
THE SWAMP MONSTERS

S o when I was about sixteen years old, best I can recall, I was staying with my Aunt Cleo while my parents were on a trip. About a week earlier my cousin, Frank, and I both had our wisdom teeth cut out and were told to stay out of the heat and sun. A few days later we took it on our own that we were fine and decided to go striper fishing, below the flood gates, at Toledo Bend Lake. That night we were camping in the back of my Toyota with a tarp spread over a rope between two trees and a Coleman light hanging in a tree limb. It got quiet, then all of a sudden, in the swamp, we heard a loud sound that got our attention fast. We both sat up and looked at each other and said, "What the hell was that?" Now we both have spent a lot of time in the woods in our life but this was a new one to us. A little later we heard it again and it was a little too much to handle so we decided spend the rest of the night sleeping inside of my truck by the highway! Ha! Ha!

Next morning, we just had to go to investigate just knowing it had to be Big Foot! We got to a huge cypress slough and there was a lot of cranes there nesting. By accident we learned that it was them making the eerie sounds. We laughed so hard at ourselves! After learning this, for years after we would bring girls, soldiers, college kids and more out there to scare the hell out of them. But it did have to be the right time of year in the summer. Some folks were so spooked that they threw their light up in the air running in fear! A lot of fun!

Chapter 27
ARKANSAS 2nd BEAR SEASON 2020

DAY ONE

It's September 24, and I lit out for my little cabin in Western Grove Arkansas. This is the first trip over twenty miles in my new Ford Raptor. I'm loving it also. I could not wait to get there. Hurricane Laura had just hit Louisiana a few weeks earlier and hit me hard she did. I was worn out from repairs and clean up. So, I'm looking forward to a little rest. Arrived at about 2 p.m. and right off had a full truck of things to unload. The first stuff out was the bait for bears down the mountain from the cabin. I put out a sack of oranges, few cans of sardines, cheap pies, dog and cat food and marshmallows covered in syrup. Placing it around different spots, the goal was to bring them in to about 25-40 yards of my stand. Hopefully, I will get a chance to sling my crossbow bolt with my new Raven R29x. Their crossbows are bad to the bone.

After a short nap, I had to get seven bags of corn and one of rice bran to my deer feeder, to start up later. So down the hill two more times with sacks of corn, so much for rest. I also trimmed a few trees. Since, I about froze last winter, I set up a box blind on a deck that I built. So now everything changed. Now there was three trees I needed to cut about the size of the top of my leg. But having only a machete I decided they would have to wait. While filling my 450-pound feeder, one bagged tipped over dumping half a bag on the ground. That was the first mistake for this bear season hunt. You are not allowed to use corn to bait until the first day of deer season. The first night was cool and would have made for perfect sleeping but the big oak, hanging over my cabin, was loaded with acorns and all night and all day it sounded like someone shooting a .22 rifle, when the acorns would hit the roof. Sucked down a bologna sandwich, a pudding and a glass of apple juice before hitting the bed.

DAY TWO

I slept in to about 7 a.m., and then made a bit of coffee and a peanut butter sandwich. I had to do a little work on the guest cabin still. I cut a hole for through the wall to install an AC, for summer and did the wiring to run off a generator. Afterwards, I made a quick hike and set out two cameras for deer. Then down the hill two more times with corn. When I approached the feeder there was a coon and a woodchuck there. I could see fresh tracks where deer had come down that night, in the spots that I had cleaned out with my foot. Now, the second mistake I made was that I forgot to spray my legs with permethrin spray and Off. So I got to fight about 150 seed ticks off of me. They are about the size of the end of a pencil making hard to see and find them. I ended up in the outdoor shower that we had built in the summer. The water was a little cool.

OPENING DAY

In my box by 6 a.m., I was excited to be hunting again and in perfect cool weather. It wasn't long before gray squirrels were scurrying on the ground. Then a few crows had to stop and put their two cents in and then came the woodchuck. After watching him consume a lot of what I had put out for bears, I almost decided to eat him. They not too bad either. The sun gradually came up and with it the heat as well. I sat to about 11:30 a.m., with not much seen.

Now I'm off to Harrison for materials and food and to pick up some firewood that I had bought this summer. I finished the afternoon shingling steps to make it safe. Then a short old man nap. I'm now 54 years old.

Back in the stand about 5 p.m. About an hour later, slowly but suddenly a black spot appeared, moving at about seventy-five yards, unbelievably quiet, through the leaves. It was a bear. A shooter also. Quickly, I got more excited than I thought I would. I just did not expect it so early. Easing my cross bow up to the window, he paused a bit looking around and came on in.

The next bad thing was instead of coming to where I had a clean shot he went to where the corn had spilled which was too high up the hill. He ate for about twenty minutes then he left, I didn't have a shot. Well, here comes that dreaded gut feeling of being sick. But I wasn't going to make a shot that I wasn't sure of. About ten minutes later he came back straight up the hill laid down like a lazy bum eating corn. Still no shot and he then left maybe thirty minutes later. Talk about sick. The season doesn't last long. The quota is 500 bears and once it is reached the season ends right then. I spent the rest of the evening hoping he would come back. Nope.

DAY THREE

Up before daylight, dripped some ole swamp water for coffee and flipped a few eggs along with it. Morning was dead still and bright from the full moon. Settled in the box stand after a quick check for unwanted critters that might have moved in, since I had left the window open. Just as the sun broke over the mountain, I heard a deer blow but too far to have been spooked by me. Owls was hooting and tooting. Slowly the light changed the paintings through the trees, color of the rocks change and just makes me feel good to be alive. For me this is an addicting peace that I can't live without. In today's times and life struggles, it is hard to find peace. At this moment I'm having a little bit of a tough time fighting a cough, that keeps interrupting my hunt.

The morning slipped by and behind me I hear a loud cough a few times. Quickly, excited, I'm reaching for my crossbow hoping for a bear. I never could see anything. I thought maybe it was the three-cow elk I had on camera. Then off my right shoulder I saw a deer and a few minutes later it ended up being eight does and yearlings. An hour later four more showed up. At 11:30, I decided to go to the cabin and eat second breakfast but as always it was good to see some animals. After a good rest and a snack, I headed down to the stand a bit early.

Down early because I needed to trim a few limbs, change camera batteries and set out a little cat food and marshmallows mixed with other goodies for some fresh smell in the wind. There was a slight breeze and temps started at about 56 degrees, pleasant. I had a few jolts when acorns slammed the top of my box stand from sixty feet above. I finished out the hunt with a lone doe coming by. Turned in for the night with sardines and crackers in hot sauce and my second fire of the year to knock the chill out.

DAY FOUR

Started out the day in the stand just at daylight belly full with a peanut butter sandwich. I called in to check the bear status, over 300 bear have now been taken. Still no bear but got to stick it out here hoping for that one shot. There is still an option to take a good buck.

After eggs for second breakfast, I feel rested enough to work on my rock walls a bit and piles of deadfall around the cabin. Then hoping to dream up a successful lure, I mixed me up some persimmon syrup, Sambuca liquor, corn, Kool-Aid powder and water in an old gallon milk jug that I hung in a tree near my stand, with hopes that a bear will catch wind of it on the mountain and come in to investigate

DAY FIVE

Broke out of bed with it windy and cool enough to layer up for the hunt. Going down the hill, there was barely enough light to see my feet and hoping the somethings that I could see was not a rattlesnake. They move a lot in October. Morning stayed cool up until the end. About 11:30 a.m., finished out seeing one squirrel and two does and two fawns. It was chilly enough to split a little wood to bring inside and build a fire in the wood stove, to warm up. After warming up and having my gut full I ended up spending a little time with my recliner.

Got in my stand a little early so I wrote some. Squirrels were late coming out but when they did it was full force. On two occasions they chatted their scared sound at each other and all split up in the trees like something approached. They don't do that often so I was hoping a bear was about to step out. I never saw a thing. About thirty minutes before dark, out of nowhere, a lone buck came out. I spent twenty minutes trying to size him as a shooter or not. I never really had that no doubt feeling. So I videoed him for friends on Facebook. He ended up staying too long though, and the more I looked at him through cross bow sights, the bigger he got. So, I eased my Raven crossbow up to and out the window on my pipe foam, real quiet, as he looked away. I leveled off on him standing where I knew he was at about 61 yards, lined circle up on him behind the shoulder, popped safety off slowly, breathed and released the bolt. Yep, a high kick and ran about fifty yards and heard him crash but could not see him. Waited about thirty minutes to go down and followed the well-made blood trail from my broad head. There he was, an eight point, no baby but not a monster. (Little ground shrinkage). Now was the fun part. I put on my rubber gloves, I always have these days, and started with the back legs, then back straps, then front legs, tenderloins and finally the neck meat and head. It took three trips up and down the mountain with my meat pack to get all the deer in the cooler. I donated all but the back straps to a veteran down the road. Too tired to cook, I scarfed up some raisin bran and hit the hay. '

DAY SIX

Not being very excited to get up this morning due to the fact that I heard three dogs barking, just down the hill, two different times and had also seen them on my text camera at my stand. So I went down the hill late. I sat until about noon and didn't see anything but about twenty-five cat squirrels.

After a little white gravy and bread, I lounged around and visited with some neighbors. Some new ones moved in that were going to end up worsening my little hunting hole with more pressure. They were more out for meat than the trophy. I understand it for sure but I never had a problem getting both in most cases and I had bought this land and built the cabin for that. But 2020 has been the worse year in my life and to make it worse after just getting done with Hurricane Laura, stomping my face in the ground, now there is another bad hurricane threat out there. Bad enough I decided to pack and fold up the chance to get a black bear. Hurricane Delta can bite me. Guess I will see. So back at the stand now for the evening hunt after taking down my tall ladder stand, alone, and humping it up the hill. Since, I've got a box stand here now, there is no need for it. At least I got one decent deer. God definitely sprinkled a little extra beauty in the Ozark Mountains and I'm blessed to share a piece of it in my lifetime. Faith, determination and want to is always best the road for me. Lazy never prevails on a good hunt or anything.

Chapter 28
ADVENTURES WITH DAVID

I have to throw in a little more about my brother David Parker. Yea see the Lord decided to change David's life at nine months old with spinal meningitis. Unfortunately, some bad doctors misdiagnosed him with the flu. By the time the mistake was discovered the fever had caused my brother to be permanently handicapped. Throughout his life, he has inspired so many especially me. He hasn't let much stop him.

So having to guess, I was around twelve years old when he wanted to run traps with me so, so bad. But with him having one leg much smaller and shorter and only one working arm, it was hard. I had always over worried over the years that he could get hurt and that held me back. However, the older we got the more I saw that God had his hand on him and always had, from four-wheeler riding, go carts, jumping hills, swimming and even one-armed bike rides with Mom. So, I determined I would let him make a round with the traps I had set out on the small creek behind our house. Usually I don't like to do this near folks home. So I had about a dozen or so traps set, from seeing trails by the water's edge, where they walk searching for crawfish and tadpoles. I used apples, sardines and dog food for bait. I was determined to have some animals for David to catch.

Like always, up before daylight both of us getting ready except this time, Mom was up as well making sure this day started out right with a quick breakfast and a quick clothes set for David. I didn't wear much back then, sometimes just a pair of shorts and rubber boots and even no socks. It was just more to worry about to dry out, if I ended up in the water. Of course, I also had a small back pack with trapping supplies and a ball peen hammer to finish off the catches. The prices for hides were decent back then and needed at that.

I had even made the time to kinda somewhat cut out a trail, hoping to help David to not trip and fall, which he did but rarely complained of it. In the woods' edge and still early enough to need a light, right off I saw eyes. We had gotten our first coon. Then a few sets down, oops, someone's house cat. When we got to it, it was mad as hell, possibly wild. There were many back then as there still are now. So ended up cutting a forked stick and pinning its head down so I could get it out of the trap. I feared one of its toes might not make it but that sucker lit out like he had grown five more toes. Now the rest of the trip was just getting through the bank's edge, with David, safe from snake bites or getting his leg caught up and twisted between roots. So we ended up with one coon and four opossums and an unwanted house cat.

Now the real story was that when we got back Mom was cooking a bigger breakfast because now my stepfather, Cullen Parker, had gotten up. So we started skinning while we waited. When Mom called us, we threw the skinned opossums up on the porch and went in to eat. We always save the meat to sell as well to an old man that wanted them all. I think he resold some of them to others. So after getting as full as pregnant armadillos, we went back out and one of the skinned opossums apparently got up and walked away with no hide! There were no dogs unchained around there and it was too big for a housecat or hawk to haul off. We guessed the old saying "playing opossum", was just that! Fickled to say the least to this day.

Chapter 29
GATOR HUNT 2021

H ello y'all. For this little story, we went down on a bayou in Palmetto Louisiana, with a friend, Casey Budden that I made back three years ago, when he got on my deer lease. We talked about setting some lines for gators since he could get tags since he owned land down there. The guy pretty much inspires me because he is having health issues that can't be figured out. Most would have quit years ago.

So, Casey put the lines out, about nine in total with number 94 line and number 12 hooks. He pulls about 30 feet of the line out and ties it good and then drapes it over a line out away from the bank where he hung it about 18 inches off the top of the water, with a good fresh chicken. The next day, we left my house in Hicks, Louisiana about 5 a.m. My girlfriend Tiffany's dad, Leo Taylor, at 70 years old, decided to go along while down visiting, from Reno Nevada. We hit Casey's drive about 7 a.m. and it wasn't long after that the boat was loaded with a few drinks, 30.30 rifle and a 17 HMR. Soon, we were putting the boat into dark dirty stained water, still as can be and lots of bubbles and leaves lying motionless atop the water. Gaping the stick steer motor back, we were off ripping through the water, Casey, Trish, Leo and me. It wasn't long before we saw the first piece of ribbon and line hanging from a cypress limb, still with bait on it. Dang!

There are always big pretty cypress trees along the bayou banks and each home you pass seems to tell a little story. Now going through the water very often a huge carp would jump out of the water, up to three-foot-high right by you and sometimes in your boat, one or ten at a time. Earlier in the week, one of Casey's buds got two ribs broken by one. A little farther down now a mile or so, carp and limb dodging, we seen the second hook stretched out tight and still. Easing the aluminum boat up to it, Casey grabbed the line and started pulling slowly up and was quick to see something jerk back. There were still a few more lines to check so we decided to let it be until we came back through. A few more lines later another one was stretched out and wrapped up in some cypress knees and on the bank the gator attached was somewhat tied up in a jam. The gator had died somehow but was still good. We were still excited especially with this first one being nine feet long. So, right off the challenge was to get this dead weight gator in the boat without tipping it. So Casey and Trish lay over on one side and me and Leo pull and drag a little at a time until we get it done. Now the bad part of this story is at 5 a.m., I had gotten a milk from a convenient store and even noticing that it was kind of warm and not quite right, I drank it anyway. So with all the exertion, I felt like I was gonna pass out and be sick and just like that too. It had to be what it was. Of course this was right in the middle of the corona virus pandemic, so that did cross my mind. Well it pretty much came and went all throughout the day.

The next line had nothing on it but the one after was straight out and we could see that a huge limb was tangled in it at the water's surface, maybe more like a tree top. Casey grabbed the line and right off we saw bubbles come up from where it was and it was trying to move away from us and the boat. Now right off Casey said that it was a good gator from the tug of the line. Both me and Casey are trying to break, snap and twist the limb out of our line all the while hoping not to get snapped. Gators can sense the slightest movement and sound. Finally, we ended up just tying the line to the front of the boat and motoring out and away from the bank, taking a risk of maybe losing it. We kept on until after about 15 minutes we freed the line. As Casey eased the line in, soon the gator saw that he was gonna be forced to the come to the top and went ballistic. Casey starts hollering, "get the 30.30!" and I'm scrambling, all along sick as hell, to find a safe shot in his giant head to plant one in the back of his skull to his brain and that I did. The more we pulled, the bigger he got. It ended up being an 11-foot 2-inch monster with a huge head. Sick or not, I was stoked to finally get a gator over ten foot and a trophy in my eyes any day. By the way, I'm trophy hunting now while I write waiting on a big buck deer that I'm after. Now, it was a good thing we were all there because it took some effort from all of us to roll the big boy over. Since all of us were on one side of the boat, it started to take in water so we had to use the gator as a counter weight. After getting our old ass selves pulled back together it wasn't long we were at the same situation again with a third gator, being ten foot. All tags filled! I guess you could say we had a boat load of gator for sure, yea! So BEAUTE, that's beautiful in the Cajun language.

So now all tagged and back to the bank, the hard part started getting them out on the ground and skinning them. Seventy degrees was coming fast and as fast as we could we were packing coolers with clean white gator meat. Gators are not only very interesting they are mighty tasty as well if cleaned right, from the moment they are taken.

Being in the place where these creatures live, in the swamp, is always a blessing of beauty, life and mystery. Till the next story "on va se revoir plus tard". That is Cajun for "we'll see each other later."
AKA Swampman

Chapter 30
FIRST BUCK CLOSE ENCOUNTER

When I was around eleven or twelve years old I was making my way to the creek on my Honda 110 three-wheeler setting my traps at a spot we called Big Bend. Here the creek made a circle and was deep enough to swim. Many kids would show up there and swim, play "Family Chase", a game from my childhood, and find a girlfriend. Back then, we were all family in our own way though. I also had my first fight here. It had a leaning tree with an old school rope tied to it with a hickory stick to hang on to. One time, my big friend Woody slung me so hard and fast that after three loops, I had no choice but to let go or hit the tree. When I did let go, it was over a thick spot where it was all rooty and a full of briars and I landed right on top of a water moccasin.

Anyway, there was a little branch that flowed off some oak ridge's down to the creek and over the years, from floods and stuff, it was probably six feet deep in some places with a shallow steady stream flowing down from it, mostly from artesian springs underground. It was a quiet evening slipping my way down the branch watching for snakes and checking and resetting my traps. I gathered beech leaves just the right size to cover my pens and traps and hid them with a little sprinkle of dirt on top and covered the sides with holly branches, which was my favorite choice. I then put two sticks on each side for them to step over, with hopes that they would put their foot right smack in the middle of the pen. No bait. You could catch most anything this way. Back then there was still a lot of foreign export and no local kill farms where folks raised fox, mink and other animals just for their hides and it was actually needed for warm clothing and more. So hides were paying pretty good and folks would eat some of what they caught as well.

While I was kneeled over one of my traps, off and on I heard beagle dogs running in the distance. They were getting close but not right on me. Then I heard something running through the leaves, over the hill where I could not see, so I stood up to look just in time as a buck deer was about to jump me in the branch. I scared him bad as he scared me accept his legs went out from under him slipping and slamming him into a tree. He stood up and looked at me and then darted off. Five minutes later the beagles came, they were running him. That six second stare down started a cause. 'Cause now I wanted to find him! At this time it had gotten easy to get my limit of squirrels with my 410 single shot gun, so now I was ready for a new challenge. From that day, it has never stopped even at 55 years old now. I will never forget that moment.

Chapter 31
TURKEY HUNT
MOULTON TEXAS

Friday March 29th

This trip started off as a six-hour drive on I-10 interstate through Houston but turned into an eight hour or more trip, after making a costly mistake of stopping at Bass Pros Sports Shop. Of course, I had to buy some things for my boat.

Finally arriving in Moulton, I got my tent all set up and went to town to get my license. I ran a few more errands and picked up some nice steaks at the local meat market to cook with Alan tonight. He is the owner of the farms that I will be hunting. I managed to find and hear some turkeys, see some deer and found some baby buzzards in an old house. Then I relaxed in the cool shade before I went out to set and try to see a hog in one of Alan's stands. Surprisingly, I wasn't there long when about nine to eleven hogs came out, mostly boars. Alan had loaned me a 300 Black Bolt Action Blackout rifle, to try out because he had been having problems with it not shooting. So, I leveled off on a nice size eating sow and squeezed. Yep, click. Dry fired. So, I ejected it and shoved in another one. This time it fired but all the pigs had heard all the commotion and was on the move. So, I think I missed but wasn't sure.

So I went to Alan's and stuffed my face and belly really good with big steaks that he grilled for us. It was easy to lay down after that for some sleep. It was a cool night and quiet. The full moon was beautiful for sure, as it crept higher in the sky through the oak limbs.

After coffee and a peanut butter sandwich, I drove to the river farm and sat and listened before daylight. It wasn't long before I heard three toms gobbling down the hill, even though it was a thick foggy morning. Sure was wishing it was opening day. So I grabbed the gun, slipped through the brush slow and easy hoping to maybe see a few pigs. With the gun over my back and a sharp shooter shovel in my hand I headed to the spring coming out of a high hill that Alan had told me he had seen what looked like arrowhead chips. No luck on arrowheads, but seen some material that showed possible sign that there could be some.

Back at camp, I scarfed down a Capri Sun and a bag of Fritos. Now, shocked I heard a faint gobble, then a couple minutes later again. Soon twenty yards from my tent was a big nice tom long beard turkey walking by, gobbling now and then. I figure looking for hens. Sorry long beard dragging sum of a gun! Gun was in the seat right next to me. That was tough. Laying in my chair with the wind massaging me now and then, in the distance I hear another faint gobble. It's killing me, having to wait. So as the sun dipped down, I grabbed my rifle and headed out to try to hear some birds roost. This way if I did, I would be set for opening day. Heard a few but with the high wind, it was tough to tell. So I never pinned any down on the roost. On the way back, in the tall grass, I spotted a pig. Slowly, easing my way trying to stay concealed behind the brush and keeping downwind, I ended up within about fifty yards of it. I raised my gun and leveled down on the pig and squeezed the shot off. The sow took a dirt nap fast. So, got a little meat in the freezer.

After, a little taco soup, I was back at the tent gazing at the moonlit sky until my head went to bobbing, so I decided to hit the hay before I crack my neck dozing. The night was cool and little breezy. I got awakened by a dang pack of yotes that sounded darn near like they was about to climb into the tent with me.

Five a.m., I was up warming water for cup of coffee and a peanut butter sandwich. I decided to go to the river to hunt because I knew where those birds had roosted. Through the gate and easing down the road in the truck as quietly as I could, with lights out, to get within 300 yards of where I heard gobblers on the roost the other morning. I started making my way through the edge of the timber, staying out of the opening to be sure I wasn't going to be seen by them. About what sounded like a mile away, I heard what I figured to be about 7 birds gobbling. They were gobbling off and on. Every now and then they were all gobbling at the same time. I could see birds chasing other birds, way out in the neighboring pasture. So I clucked, purred and cackled but just could not get any ole tom off the hens. But that's normal early. So awhile went by and suddenly, I started having one gobble a good bit closer and now and then it gets even closer. Sure enough, like a ghost, a tom appeared a few feet across the neighbor's fence. He had seen my hen decoy and Funky Chicken Jake. A jake is a young gobbler. Sadly, it was too small of a bird, maybe two years old with a four-inch beard. But still fun to watch. But my luck was changing especially being Easter Sunday. The small bird had drawn the attention of a bigger bird that came in and ran him off. Like the smaller bird, he was hung up on the fence because it was grown up with tall grass and briars. Suddenly, he disappeared. A couple of minutes later, he showed up but this time on the right side of the fence. I drew a bead on his head at about thirty yards and he made a drop kick approach to die, for turkey dressing. Thank God, He has risen and saved me by His grace, so that I may live amongst his awesome creations until my final day has come. Love my Lord and Savior.

Now setting timer on my phone, I got a few pics and then headed to Alan's to show him and get the big boy on ice. He was toting about an eleven-and-a-half-inch beard, some nice spurs and had to be 25 or 27 pounds. We celebrated with grilled chicken later at Dairy Queen in Hallettsville before my nap.

First day of April, and Easter was once again seen through my eyes as to how awesome God is. Everything is so green from the rains past and the flowers and the smell in itself is amazing right now. Life was buzzing allover with springtime in full bloom. While dozing, I was awakened by some faint gobbles in the distance, so I headed down hill about 200 yards and set up. Right off, I was answered by three gobbles and thirty minutes later or so two big hens came in cackling. Sure enough, four long beards were following and came within thirty yards of the decoys. It would have been nice to have a shooter. Back to camp, I was quick to make a Mountain House meal, brush my teeth, clean my dishes and flop off into my sleeping bag.

The next morning, I decided to go out for fun again one more time and maybe try to make a live video on Facebook, for my friends. An hour before daylight, I heard a gobble and headed that way. As the steadily rising sun broke the tree line, more and more birds began to liven up which helped make the turkeys gobble, every fifteen minutes or so. Which helped me move in closer. Hawks, owls and crows always get them to gobble a lot. Soon, I had gotten to what I figured was 200 yards from the tree line edge, of a big pasture, where it sounded like they were. Unfortunately, this was the neighbor's land. Yelp sure enough they had pitched down there. All I could do was watch them strut, chase hens and work their way farther from me and go in the wrong direction. It was good to see as always though.

So back to camp and pack up to head off through Yoakum, to Cuero Texas to a new spot, Haun Ranch owned by Mr. Terry. I've never been there so thought I'd give it a try. I got there about 11 a.m., and met him at the lodge. Two other guys were coming in from Pennsylvania, a twenty-hour drive, to hunt pigs. Out before daylight, I was feeling a bit energized after a good night rest and a shower. I heard a vague gobble off in the distance but not long enough to be able to tell from which way. I waited a bit, hoping to hear another and usually so, but not this morning. With a wild guess, I walked on in even though my instincts said to stay put. Got the decoys out and chair set up and started calling with a slate call. Yelp, yelp, yelp, still no return. An hour or so passed and every thirty minutes the wind seemed to increase. A few deer passed by and then like a ghost, a lone hen popped out at about 400 yards away. I was kinda surprised that she was alone. My guess is that she was already nesting and got up to feed a bit quickly. About twenty minutes later, kinda to my hard right, a heard a faint gobble. Soon there was a red head rubbernecking my way. He stopped at about fifty yards and started strutting and drumming behind some brush. Dang! This went on about fifty yards from my decoys. He just seemed not to want to come out of the brush, all long making me antsy. Eventually, he moved about two feet. Geeze! I had thought I had a big enough window through the limbs to make the shot. So, I waited until he came out of his strut and stuck his head out, then I aimed and squeezed the trigger. Bam! Man I missed! I shot two more times at him running off unloading my gun. Sick, sick, sick. Looking between limbs I think he was a bit farther than I had thought. I can honestly say, I have no idea how long it has been since I have done that. I reckon the stars just weren't lined up to take that big boy. It was a nice mature tom. So, I've got one more stop to make and I'm headed back to Louisiana if I don't get one there.

Now it's about an hour twenty-minute drive down to Earnest Metting's farm, on the bank, of a little river, full of scattered oaks. This is a four-bird county which is the best part allowing me to hunt longer which I did and was successful. I sat down on the edge of the road where it made a tee, on a big long flat, where I had seen a big tom's tracks where he had been dragging his wing tips in the sand. After calling a while and working up the crows, I heard a gobble close. I hit the call one more time, about five minutes went by and dang near right behind me he gobbles and walks out, kinda to my right, and sees me. So I took the only shot I probably was gonna get at him there, and it was good. Bad thing was that it blew off most of his beard, being too close. Either way, I had some turkey jerky coming and enough left to stink up some grease later. These hunts have been a blessing and I feel blessed that these men, Earnest, Alan and Dustin, share their places with me that they have worked hard on their whole lives, I'm fond of all these men and consider them family because they make me feel that way, sharing their land with me.

Chapter 32
SQUIRREL HUNTS AS KIDS

This story is about a hunt my cousin, me and our Uncle Jerry Dale Williams went on. When he took us most of the time, it was with my Uncle Huey Williams and two dogs Jack and Bowser. We were never cut any slack to keep up or catch up either and we would have to carry the squirrels. Now Frank had gotten a new fancy hunting vest with a pouch in the back and this day we filled it up with fox and cat squirrels. Back at grandma's we skinned them out on a nail driven in the big oak out in the back. The dogs got all the heads to chew on and the guts for snacks. Sometimes you would get to smell and hear the first ones skinned cooking before the last ones were skinned with a few eggs maybe.

So Frank forgot one small one in the vest and went home. Days later his closet was rank and his mom, my Aunt Cleo, tore his room up trying to figure it out. She found the rotting corpse in his vest and made him do the cleanup.

Chapter 33
FIRST DEER HUNT RED OAK OKLAHOMA 2021

DAY ONE

Hello Y'all. I've been excited to see what would become of this hunt. I've dreamed all my life to find the time and place of my own, to maybe get some 140 inch to 170-inch deer. So, I seen this five-acre place on the internet and from looking on Google Earth and the onX

Hunt app, it seemed to be in a good spot. Now, we had just been to look at another spot over the mountain in Talihina, on the other side of the Ouachita Mountains but the guy ended up backing out of the sale a few weeks prior. The guy sure enough had enough sign of big bucks there and pictures to back it up, and straight as the crow flies it was only about six miles across to it, on Google Earth. So I ended up buying the five acres which is much smaller than the 100 acres I've dreamt of. It's a beautiful place full of little oaks and cedars. The bottom half is flat with a small seasonal stream and gradually goes up a hill at about 45 degrees. There is nothing but woods on three sides and a small cattle farm in front with a great road so I figured its land, so I can't lose buying it.

So before even buying it, I was laying out a trail using ripped Walmart bags, for a future dozer to cut a path in for a stand, place to park and a food plot. Also ran out to buy some mineral licks. We then go back to our kayak trip in Arkansas and we made a plan for some money to lock it down with the owner.

So now that I own it, I get a dozer out and had some rock spread. A month or so went by and it was time to figure out how I was going to hunt it. After a bunch of ideas, I ended up building an 8x14 foot hunting cabin that would be both to sleep in and hunt in. This time lumber was higher than I had ever seen it due to Hurricane Laura and the corona virus pandemic. So using about half of materials that I had and buying the rest, I came out with a nice one for the job. It was fully insulated and had double paned windows. Built, then delivered and set up by myself on location in less than 30 days. Everything was pretty smooth until on the trip home when I realized that I had lost one of my ramps from my trailer. On this trip we also set up a feeder and a cell camera that could be a whole other story, but ended up getting one to finally work. Tiffany and I spent a few hours with a chainsaw clearing shooting lanes and taking trees out where need be without over doing it and planted a food plant then hoped for the best.

Back home waiting, it took longer than I had hoped to finally see some good bucks on my text camera. One was pushing 170 inches which made me kinda happy. A nice black bear also showed up leaving me with the worry that it tore up my feeder. I did end up back there one more time just to reset cameras and make sure the feeder was working and doing small things that I had forgotten needed done.

Fast forward a few months. Now it is October 28 2021 and with a decent ten-day weather forecast, with temps dropping, I left home at 5 a.m. and I was unpacking, in the rain, by 1 p.m. Sure enough temps had dropped and so did the rain, all day this day, with wind gusts of 40 mph.

I made the first evening hunt and ended up seeing a few does and realized that I should have parked my truck in the back away from the cabin. They did not like the new object and knew that it shouldn't be there. Here alone with no water or electric, dark came fast. Under a light, I made macaroni and cheese and soon hit the cot. I was looking at ten plus hours until I wake up for the first morning hunt. The night's sleep was rough with winds whipping and blowing things atop my tin roof waking me up. This was on top of my usual multiple awakenings that I experience every night.

DAY TWO

Daylight now kinda looking at me through the blinds, I ended my second bowl Cap'n Crunch, after slipping outside to get the milk, quietly. Finished up a cup of instant coffee, dressed for the cold temps, about 45 degrees I guessed, and loaded my ass in the office chair. I then eased the window open, sprayed down and got my Raven crossbow cocked and loaded. I was peering through the trees out into the woods. It was rough but beautiful hunting weather and I was feeling blessed. Thanks all to the Almighty God. It didn't take long to see all the animals that were blessed by the corn that I was feeding. A beautiful fox came by, squirrels chasing all about, crows dodging trees to the ground and red birds were all around. Thank God to all the farmers who help feed us and the wildlife. It took a while but soon I got a glimpse of movement, on the forest floor through the trees of what I was looking for, it was a deer. I was hoping to get that extra heartfelt rush of seeing a big rack of antlers. Each are unique to their own like human finger prints, in most cases. However, this time it ended up being two does with two yearlings, one being a real big doe. Buck never showed but two did show up on the cameras this night. The new text cameras have been a game changer for both excitement and disappointment. The best part is the amount of times that we left our stands to go home and then the buck we were after would show up on camera.

That night I scarfed down a can of world-famous Vienna sausage with bread and creole seasoning. Slop food. Then I hugged up to my cot and together we slept well in the chilly little cabin.

DAY THREE

Cap'n Crunch, coffee and a Capri Sun and daylight was here. I cut my buddy heater off and eased my window open and it felt like someone threw cold air in my face. So I grabbed my little blanket and slid it over my legs, eased back, said my prayers and watched the party begin right off with squirrels. It sure is a big difference from my younger days, of a two mile plus trek in the middle of nowhere, then hiking up a tree with a climber, to wait on big boy. Also, a big change from sleeping in an old army sleeping bag rolled up in a small tarp with a pad of small leaves and branches to help keep the cool air off. It was a perfect morning in the 40's and dead calm. A few hours later, eight does and yearlings showed up and stayed for about 20 minutes then slowly headed back the way they came out. The good news is that it seems a few more has joined the group but the bad news is no bucks. Also, that is that much more that I will have to feed to keep them around.

For the evening hunt, I went up the hill a bit to my 22-foot ladder stand that I got set up on my second day here. It started out still and quiet but then my neighbor came out to get some cedar trees that he had cut down, for posts. He ended up having trouble with his truck. So, the motor started revving, doors slamming and some curse words started flying. What sounded like a pack of hounds in the bed of his truck didn't help either. Well I did get a break on my stand, a buck was there on my camera with a giant rack on one side and a spike about eight inches long with a small hook on the other. This was definitely a cull buck messing up the gene pool. I scarfed down some soup and got to bed. It didn't take long before the frigid night air made the inside of the cabin cold fast. The top of my head and hair was very, very chilly. Now, it was nine to ten hours until daylight with no phone, no TV, no body, no animals, no power, nothing but dead quiet that was enough to hear your guts work and your heart beat. It's the kind of solitude that gives yea time to think good, soul search, clear your head, cleanse yea heart and just flat out be honest with yea self on what needs to be changed to better yourself, find forgiveness in yea heart and let things go. A person can't hide from his own heart and soul, they know the things God knows. Many a man has saved himself through the years in different ways by going out in the wilderness. So have I.

DAY FOUR

The morning was good and chilly. After downing a little oatmeal. I eased into my chair and closed the curtains behind me to hide the rest of the cabin. It wasn't long until a few does come by with their yearlings. It is always interesting to see the yearlings interact with each other and the rest of the animals. Meantime, some good deer are being taken at home, but none like what I've had on camera here, which is why I am trying here. Next thing I knew noon had come around and deer had come and gone. So, I choked down some beanie weenie sausage with beans and bread and a Capri Sun drink. After all the bobbing up and down that my head was doing trying to stay awake, my neck was hurting bad, so I swallowed four Motrin's and laid down. It hurt to even lay on it. The day grew warmer and overcast, quiet, calm and still. Sleeping off and on, the whole time I knew that this was a good day for a buck to move from my experience of days in the past. Also, as a plus, up behind me on the hill, there were two pawings, scrapes, made on the ground. Additionally, down in front of my box stand, I had hung a dripper in a tree full of Tink's 69 deer lure and I cleared the ground under it creating a mock scrape. The dripper was above the limb just off the ground. Neck pain or no, I had laid there long as I could stand with too much rest. Ten plus hours of time in a cot is rough enough. I don't hang around outside because outside is my hunting area. To be dead quiet at night and not to go to and from my stands are all a part of my strategy for this spot although it does make it rough. Now, I was thinking how bad it would be to put this much work into a spot and not even see a buck and what a hard row to hoe that would be and swallow.

Now about 4:10 p.m., I got up eased my boots on quietly and moved around my cabin for a drink of water. I decided to pull back the black curtain that separates the blind from the sleeping area, and take a peek out of the window. There was a lone deer out there with a big body. I could not quite see the front of it or the head from a cluster of live oak trees. Soon, it made one step and I could see antlers. Now as quick as I could and as quiet as I could, I sat down cocking my crossbow and eased up my window, which I was sure was going to get me busted. After managing through, I saw that it was a shooter. Because I didn't want to make a bad shot I got out the range finder, now risking time though. I had guessed 50 yards and it was actually 45. I leveled my crossbow in the window waiting for him to step forward and open up the area between his front legs. Wow, this was all so perfect. I thought to myself "I can't mess this up". I aimed a tad high with my forty-yard circle crossbow scope and squeezed the trigger. Thump, and a high kick. I watched him run through the food plot into the thicket with what looked like blood on his side. So, now pumped and nervous as always, with the possibility of losing an awesome animal which is rare but happens occasionally, I decided to give him 30 minutes. Looking too early might make him run more. However, I did ease out to where I had shot him to recoup my arrow. Right off I was fickled because there wasn't any blood, really, on my shaft except but a speck but it was wet with body fluid. No hair or blood was visible. Damn, was that blood that I had seen on him? So I had to walk in the same direction he ran. Thirty yards out I started seeing a trail of blood but not like I had hoped. Worry, worry, worry. I walked back to the cabin grabbed some water and got my crossbow recocked and loaded and eased back out to the blood trail. Now, I'm slipping along the blood trail like a cat after its prey and readying myself in case this deer did not go down but instead lay wounded and should try to kill me. I was using anything under my feet to help me stay quiet. After a 120 yards or so, the blood staying the same, I again worry. Ahead 50 yards or so, I see the road, scanning all around me as I move towards it, I see nothing. Damn! Now up to the road I see specks of red across it. Then across the road, 25 yards into the woods, I see white. I raised my crossbow to take advantage of the four-power scope. I was sure it was a deer. But I wasn't sure if he was dead or alive. I eased across the road, crossbow leveled out the whole time, but by God's grace and blessings, he was dead. He was a beautiful eight point with a tall perfect rack. Ending and starting what I hope is the beginning of many stories like this, on my new little piece of land, in the Oklahoma Mountains.

Thankfully, there are days of feeling like hope is still there especially during the time of this year 2021. Thanks to God and a good hunt to make most days better. Oh, how I love God for the good ones and how He helps me out through the bad ones. Never stop till you drop! Bow up till yea throw up if have to, to get what you want. On another note now I'm up to 55 acres there through God's help building the dreams and memories. THANK YOU LORD;

Chapter 34
IRELAND 2022

This trip started the year before in 2021, with me just wanting to get out of the heat in Louisiana and chase a species I never have before, in a foreign land. So Sika deer it was in Ireland. Also, it is a place my girl, Tiffany, had always wanted to go so that made it even better.

So, after buying the plane tickets, we were really excited and ready to go, but then we were told that we needed to get the Covid vaccine shot. Not us and not yet so we cancelled. We knew more people that got sick with it than without it, and who never got sick. It was too fast, too soon.

Now 2022 September 14, we boarded the plane from Alexandria Airport to Atlanta for a six-hour layover. Finally, we're up in the air for eight more hours before landing in Dublin, Ireland. There we got a taxi to The Bonnington Dublin hotel and could not wait to rub up to the bed, having no sleep at all on the jet and the time change was rough too.

The next morning we were picked up by an associate of Martin Curran, the outfitter, who took us to our lodging at the Woodford Dolmen, in Carlow. After settling in we set out to check our guns out, at 500 yards. That evening we went out on the first hunt in Ireland for Sika deer. Sika are the smallest deer species in Ireland. Ireland was lush with vegetation and beauty. Everything was very clean, we rarely seen any trash along the roads and the roads were in great shape pretty much. It felt like I was on a go cart ride driving through the narrow roads lined with rock fences and walls and shrubs full of flowers. The fields were flooded with cattle, sheep and more sheep.

Now down the mountain, we ended up leaning against a rock wall, made no telling how long ago. As they cleared fields and farms years ago, they moved rocks to build fences and to make land markers. You seem them everywhere, some are as old as Ireland herself. We were glassing with binos, into Wicklow Forest located in the County Wicklow, which is known as the "Garden of Ireland" for its magnificent scenery. It was easy to see where God had sprinkled extra beauty here. It wasn't too long before we spotted one small stag, male Sika, with eleven hinds, females, scattered just above the tree line. He wasn't big enough to stalk though so we backed out and went to a farm. We started into it but got busted by two hinds. We then climbed up into a big tree stand that I could tell had been there for some time. After 45 minutes or so, a spike came out from the tree edge of the field and fed a long time by itself. An hour or so later, I began to shake from the cold. I had been used to real hot temperatures at home. Burr… shaking. Then right at dark, a six point and a spike came out and I dropped both. The shaking wasn't helping my confidence any, so glad that I got it done. I shot the spike because the landowner had wanted some meat. Now, that I'm getting older, it didn't take long to warm up dragging them up the hill to the truck.

Second Day

We drove a bit farther to Hacketstown, allowing me to see more of this beautiful place. They drive on the opposite side of the road than us in the USA, so it takes a little getting used to. Just before daylight, we worked our way up a hundred yards at a time, stopping to get a breath then go again. Slowly, through tall trees, we broke out on a huge opening where we could see for miles. We were just in time to see the sun come up to paint those pictures that you never forget. There was a light breeze and cool enough to need a light coat, a long sleeve shirt and a hat over your ears. When we sat down, I kind of wished I had worn long johns though. Smelling the fresh cut grass, I couldn't help envy people living on the farms way off in the distance, knowing they probably never felt closed in.

Soon, I caught some movement on the skyline, it was a beautiful red fox with a full coat, not like the ones we see at home. They shoot them here but I had to pass, I just wanted to watch him or her, in my binos as long as I could. Even as cautious as we were, we were seen by four deer over the horizon, so we darted down into a deep cut in the mountain. With some fast walking and a little jogging, we got up far enough to see them. Now pretty much winded, gun on shooting sticks, trying to get steady, I squeezed off a shot. Martin liked the shot. First shot was a hit but the next few we thought missed but not with all of them. The stag dropped into tall brush and grass but then picked up his head and all we could see were his antlers. The shot was 706 yards according to my Leica binoculars with built in range finder, making it my longest shot ever. I guess a couple of long-range tips Martin had given me that he had learned from a Ukraine sniper, might have helped. Trying to get another shot we stalked 400 yards, then 250 yards but nothing. We ended up making a circle under the ridge and sneaking up to him within 25 yards and popped him in the neck to finish him off. I was stoked for sure to have ended and started another adventure. Dragging the stag up and down the mountain was rough, dead weight behind a rope. I could have been happy to debone him and pack out just the meat but I guess it's kind of part of it for them.

Going through town, we hit one of the few McDonald's there and got our cholesterol on with some fat building materials. Then on to drop the meat off at the meat cooler. Tiffany had gone to do some sightseeing with Martins girl, Elaine. Well, I wasn't expecting it to happen so fast but it was a nice eight point and good enough for a true free range Ireland deer. On the drive to the motel, I noticed many turnabouts. Recycling is serious here and there are hardly any trucks except work trucks. Also, the street signs were large and easy to see. Every house and yard was kept up and pristine. The primary religions seem to be Catholic and Presbyterian.

The second evening hunt, Tiffany went with and we rode around the area a lot, getting out now and then and glassing. Walking without worry because there are not any snakes or predators pretty much here. However, they are not without spiders, ticks, mosquitoes and more. Goats, Sika deer, Red Stagg and Fallow Deer as well as domestic animals are spread out everywhere. On a side note, unlike the USA, you have to be financially independent and meet all the conditions to retire here if you are not a citizen. Food portions seem small here for the most part and not much ice is served in your drink.

Back to the hunt. We got up the next morning and scarfed down breakfast and waited for Lance to pick us up for the second half of the hunting trip. It was a three and a half over drive to Donegal, to our new room at the Mount Errigal Hotel, with anticipation of a Red deer. Now it's time to catch up on a bit of sleep.

The next morning we caught ourselves out before daylight slowly making our way up through the hills, behind some big farms, and then perched up on a big rock overlooking the hills. Again, I feel blessed to see another sunrise. Sitting, I was taking in all the beauty and getting a little chilly. We moved on up and over the mountain. Soon we spotted some goats that looked to be Spanish Ibex and Mouflon maybe. These are not native and can be hunted year-round. They weren't what I was after though. Up and moving again, we spotted three hinds on the ridge about a thousand or so yards straight across. After watching for twenty minutes or so, we saw a bull. We could tell he was no giant but nothing to slouch at either. So, we made a plan to swing around, out of the wind, in hopes that the bull would still be just over the mountain ridgeline, where they had disappeared. We then eased over the ridge and got sat down. It was thick and we couldn't see very far. Then to our surprise, we heard a roar in the timber. We were surprised at this because it was so early in the season. When I booked this hunt, I knew it was a bad time to go so early in the season but we had things at home to do later on in the year. Short time later, out of nowhere, he was a 100 yards away, in front of me but I could not see him. Tiffany spotted him first. I was looking out further not expecting him to come in so close. When I did spot the bull, I could barely see him through the limbs in the scope. I decided to not pass on the first day on something I might not see, with only having three days to hunt, so I gambled and squeezed the trigger where I thought it was best. Just like that, it ran to my left and disappeared, so I jumped up running that way hoping to get another shot. Sure enough he had stopped and he and I saw each other at the same time. As he was running away, on the third hop, I took him down. Short and sweet and rare, I was relieved that I had gotten it over already with a nicer free range eight point. It was also nice to have my lady with me this round. We spent the next few days looking for a bigger one but only saw a few smaller bulls and hinds.

I just decided to cut all the antlers off at the skulls and clean the burs really good, making sure there wasn't any hair and meat left on them, in order to get them to USA and we did. Now off to the touring part, so we got up a bit later. For the next few days, we toured the scenic countryside stopping at many historical and breathtaking sites. On the first day we visited a few old churches where we always said a prayer and gave a donation. Architecture of these century old buildings are as beautiful as they are astonishing that they have survived for centuries. We also visited a castle ruin and old cemetery with headstones that were dated as early as the 1800's. Later, we were awe-struck by the second highest cliffs in Ireland, the Slieve League on the Atlantic coast. We visited other castles, national parks, fishing ports and a place called Glencolmcille folk village. Here the town is set with cottages from centuries ago, with each one depicting a different period with artifacts from that era. Along the way, we learned many interesting facts about the country during the drive. For instance, crossbow hunting is not allowed. Houses average 300-700 thousand dollars on the average. Sheep are spray painted to keep up with whose is whose because they all look alike. Some of the finest blackberries I have ever seen and they were everywhere! So I made my goal to treat myself. So glad God gave me the means to visit this magical spot-on Earth.

Chapter 35
COKE CAN OKLAHOMA 2022

T his adventure started with just looking for a place with a better class of deer. A few years back, I worked hard and tried in the Ozark Mountains on the Buffalo River, near Harrison, in a town called Western Grove Arkansas. I had an awesome little cabin built with a lot of deer around. Then Chronic Wasting Disease set in. I went from seeing an average of fifteen deer a day to maybe two a week, after only a few years.

So determined not to quit, I started looking in Oklahoma. I'm trying to stay seven hours or less drive from the house. I saw an ad for five acres on the internet and by the sight of the interactive map, I could tell that it had a possibility for good deer, and if not any land was worth the work. So, I went to look at it and decided to give it a try. Dreams can start small. The hardest thing is just getting started. The price started out at 25 grand but I got it down to 18 with three thousand down, owner financed. Before the deal was even signed, I set up a mineral site and flagged off an area for a dozer work to set up a food plot and stand site. My original thought was to bring an older RV I had but I quickly changed that idea to building a small cabin big enough to hunt, sleep and camp out of. I did have a bit of worry that it would spook the deer though. Ended up building an 8x14 cabin and hauled it up on my track hoe trailer a few months later. However, this story is mainly about the second half of this idea. The cabin did work out great all the way around and I took a nice eight point for my first buck with this idea.

Fast forward a little longer than a year, when a neighbor mentioned to me that five more acres had come up for sale right by me. I had to buy it, even though I had to borrow money to do it. Rough! At this same time a guy I had met earlier, had his 15 acres up for sale. He is the only guy past me for miles through the woods. All of this was happening while I was making a motor cycle trip of over a thousand miles with a few friends. There was no way I was gonna be able to buy his fifteen acres, so I threw out to him that I had a decent house back home to trade him for it. I made him the offer after he told me that he was selling because he was tired of off grid living. He had started a cabin and it was about half way through. We ended up making the trade for the house and eight acres that I had for his fifteen acres. After a ton of cleaning up the whole place that was filled with trash and junk, including an old RV and having a skid steer out three times, I was ready to hunt.

I returned about a week after bow season opened. This was not intended. I had hired a guy to work on finishing my cabin and after paying him 1500 dollars he ended up in jail. Consequently, causing me to have to do the work myself. Luckily, he had brought out a few materials. While I was there I hunted in the mornings, evenings and during the day.

Second night there, I got a picture of a ten point, I called crab claw. This deer and I went toe to toe last year but I could never catch him out before dark. So, the game was set. Temps were really perfect around the 40's in the mornings and 50's in the evenings. The leaves were starting to change. There had been one of the worst droughts in many years here, and the deer had struggled hard throughout the summer making obvious why the buck's antlers had not changed much from last year. Since, there weren't any acorns to be found, I had pulled does from most every bait site. Across the road on five acres, up in the mountains, I set up a ground blind and brushed it in really well. It was thick there with a lot of cedars scattered about with rocks. I had seen a few decent bucks off and on. The next day, after about an hour in my chair, like a ghost, to my right, a lone doe slowly appeared. About the time she came into full view, she spooked a bit when a dozen squirrels heard a hawk and split in every direction. A minute later, in the same spot, I could see white antlers coming through the woods. I reached slowly for my Raven cross bow that was leaned up against the blind wall and eased it up into the blind window where I had a piece of parachute cord tied to rest my cross bow on, for a steady shot. He stopped dead at a tree that I had ranged to be at 40 yards. So, I set the circle on the deer about an inch behind his shoulder and an inch high and squeezed the trigger. Thump and jump and ran back about twenty yards laying there kicking in the leaves but still looked lively so I bolted out rushing to re cock the crossbow and made another shot to be sure. I was so happy that it was Crab Claw. He was a little better than what I had expected. So I am very happy with my first hunt. I ended up being gone about 40 days hunting and working on the cabin, stands and food plots.

Now back home to Louisiana for a few weeks hunting. Tiffany ended up getting a big bodied seven point and I got took a nice eight point. I saw the temps were going to drop in Oklahoma. My place is between Talihena and Red Oak Oklahoma. For a few days off and on I started packing up my truck with hunting gear and tools. I left out about four a.m. and ended up getting to my place around one p.m.

On the way up, I made a stop at my first stand to change batteries, bait and check camera cards. A few shooter bucks had been there that anyone would be proud to take but not the, over 160-inch, monster I am still praying will show up. I know they are around because I have seen pictures from folks that live only five to ten miles around me. It never hurts to keep dreaming and trying. Up at the new cabin, I did the same thing just baiting and getting ready. I placed new propane bottles in my new Muddy box stand and the cabin, and just in time. By dark, I was digging for my long johns to put on and a heavier coat. Right off that evening where we had planted a food plot, I saw deer. Also, here is where I had my fist picture of my target buck for my last deer tag. It was an eight point my neighbor called Coke Can. It was the second time this season that my toes got cold.

First night it was quick to see that I wasn't going to freeze in the new cabin. It would have helped to have a wood burning stove because I could not afford to burn propane all night. So early to bed buried down in sleeping bad with a quilt all night made for some long nights. I did manage to get a gas stove in to help with the cooking. I used the solar light that I kept outside during the day inside for light as well as the lights that use batteries. I used my 2000-watt generator a few hours in daylight to recharge anything that needed it. First night was 28 degrees Burr.

Next morning waking up to an ice cube with ground frozen, it wasn't hard to lay back down and wait for the sun to come up to go hunt. I've never had the best of luck early on, on real cold mornings. So at about eight a.m., I slipped down to my stand looking like the Pillsbury Dough Boy with all my heavy clothes on. I hadn't been there too long when the bit of sunlight faded into overcast with a little chillier wind and then a bit of sleet. Quickly, I was entertained by squirrels everywhere. A hawk flew by gawking at them sending fear through their little bodies a few times. Later a few Red Headed Woodpeckers appeared for pecking away for their breakfast. Soon the sleet turned into a pretty heavy snow that quickly turned the ground into a white blanket. Already I could see that this was gonna be one of those days. Cold or not God gives you a reason to be alive. It was super quiet. Soon a huge gobbler, first I had seen here, comes by. Knowing they had a fall season, I considered taking him but I didn't know the full details so I decided to pass. Then the deer started moving bucks and does with some of them chasing which gave me a clue that I might have hit it right for the rut. All critters were out on what most would see as the worst day for man or beast to be out. After experiencing a terrible drought they seemed to be filled with happiness from the relief from ticks, mosquitos and biting flies. I sure was.

The evening hunt wasn't much different no shooter showed. The nights were like most in that your regrouped, ate and prepared for the next morning and then got into bed where it was warm. It was just you and the quiet so the body and mind could heal. I use a lot of this time to reflect on my past and my future, thinking about the things that I need to improve on and things I need to get rid of, my attitude and most of all to pray more. So fast forward through another six more days of temps in the mid-forties in daytime and mid-twenties at night. My toes were never warm. I swear the cold gets worse on me, the older I get. I did make the time to do a few things but overall any extra work got put on the back burner due to the cold and shorter days. I pretty much spent seven hours a days just sitting. Aggravating and rough some times, but kind of what it is all about. It is not the killing or even the meat so much as just the challenge of hunting your target buck and then the blessing you receive after taking him. Not just any buck, *the* buck. It's the one you watched grow on camera, lost sleep trying to get, sacrificed time from home, work and family hunting him. Sometimes persevering three to four years in your efforts of taking the trophy. In my case spending thousands of dollars to buy land in order to pursue my passion and dreams. Every man needs something else to work for besides what he has to work for, anyway. It can be done. Hard work and clean living, with God Almighty having yea back, the best help of all.

So today is about the tenth day with it actually warming back up to about 40 degrees the last few evenings. I headed to the stand up the mountain, named Thick Hill Stand, because the ground blind there has one hole about ten inches round to look out of down a three foot by forty-yard path. It is not for most people. It is only a small spot to bait with a natural food source there being acorns. As the season progresses, the bucks grow smarter, leerier and move less in the daylight, so I go to cover. This evening was for sure when my hope started to get low and I was mentally and physically tired from the hunt. Everyday less and less deer were showing up and now I had a dang guy with his dad, brother and a friend hunting right across the road from me not 150 yards from my stand, even though they had 54 acres to hunt on. Which is kind of sad since I've spent so much on baiting that spot for them to practically be on top of me. Nothing I could do. Everyday friends are getting good bucks here and there which make me happy and a little sad, kinda. Just then I get a text from Kenny, a new friend from Oklahoma, he just got a huge buck. Ten minutes later, I hear a gunshot right about where my stand was, where those guys were hunting so closely. Gun season had just opened a few days earlier. So, I texted the guy hunting across the road and he told me that his dad had shot and taken a nice one. Now, my spirits are down even more. That guy hadn't even spent two hours hunting before he got this deer. That is the way it goes sometimes though but it didn't help me none with my hunt. I figured with my luck he probably got Coke Can. I got down to the point where I almost left the stand early and I even dropped my crossbow down to the corner of my blind and started to put a few things away in my pack. Kind of moping now, with my head down, looking at the ground when a squirrel ran up a tree barking and whipping his tail making me look up to see a deer body coming through the woods. Grabbing my bow and getting ready, I was shocked that it was Coke Can. A little worked up more than usual, I let him get to my 40-yard mark and make the shot with about 30 minutes of daylight left. A few minutes later, I walked out to where he was standing…no blood. At first my heart sank then ten yards out, I found my bolt with blood on it from one end to the other, what looked like lung blood. So feeling a little bit better, I decided to wait until dark to start my tracking.

I was trying to be quiet as a mouse but no way could be that quiet but I tried best I could with my headlight and my blood light. First I was a little sickly after not seeing the blood that I hoped to see, because usually I do see blood, that's even if they go one step after being hit. Inching along to the point where I even lost the blood trail but then found some heavy blood loss from him with it continuing all along the way until I seen him lying there. A sick dizzy feeling fell over me and it was like I was being picked up by a crane now that I knew he was down. Quickly, I was on my knees with this beautiful animal praying thanking God for the harvest and this big buck's soul. Then the work started. I left a small red light high in the tree where he lay after gutting him and quickly returned to camp for my meat pack. I hoped to beat the coyotes back to him. I was alright. He was a full load packed out down the ridge to the four-wheeler.

Thank God for this hunt and this place and most of all for the health to do it. I spent a lot of the night and early the next morning packing to head home to see my lady, Tiffany, who works so hard to see me get to enjoy my addiction and passion, for the love of the hunt. Find yours and keep God in it. Nature is there with love.

Sincerely Swampman

www.ingramcontent.com/pod-product-compliance
Lightning Source LLC
Chambersburg PA
CBHW041626140626
46547CB00030B/1066